# TRACEABILITY TECHNOLOGY

# For

# Food Manufacturers

# Traceability Technology

## For Food Manufacturers

How to be Ready for Blockchain

Judith Kirkness

Canada, 2019

Cover: Josh Guidi

# Table of Contents

# Chapter 1. Because you have to

Traceability is not a new concept in business. Some industries have been doing serial or lot number traceability for decades. One example is the vehicle identification number (VIN) found on every vehicle. VIN's were introduced in 1954. In 1979 and 1980, the VIN number format was standardized by the ISO (International Organization for Standards) and now all vehicle manufacturers use the same 17-character format. Decoding the VIN can tell you what manufacturer, in what country, produced that vehicle as well information such as the model year, a description of the body type and the plant that manufactured it.

This kind of traceability is now common in many other industries including electronics, consumer packaged goods and of course, food. For example, using an online guide, you can decode your iPhone serial number to learn the model, colour, country it was manufactured, machine the device was produced on, storage size as well as the year and week of manufacture.

In the food industry, the European Union made traceability compulsory for food manufacturers in 2002. In North America, demonstrating traceability for the purposes of recall is a requirement for qualifying for Global Food Safety Initiative (GFSI) certification schemes such as SQF (Safe Quality Food), BRC (British Retail Consortium) and FSSC 22000 (Food Safety System Certification). Traceability is also a requirement for satisfying Canadian Food Inspection Agency (CFIA) and Food and Drug Administration (FDA) inspection (Canada). As a result, most food manufacturers have some form of traceability already.

While I know from working for over 20 years with food manufacturers that they are committed to producing safe food for consumers, I have found that many companies still view traceability technology and tracking as a 'cost' of doing business in today's marketplace.

**What many business owners and managers don't recognise is that they could be using the information collected for traceability purposes beyond recall, to better monitor and understand their business. Better information allows for more informed decision making and can help you become more profitable.**

This book was written to help all you who process or manufacture food or consumer packaged goods. It will help you understand how to tackle electronic traceability tracking and in doing so offer useful information that can help you save money, understand your true costs, evaluate your yields and reduce shipping errors. If you have adapted your business to track the information needed for recall and if the only benefit you are receiving is inspector approval, you are missing an opportunity that could be giving you an edge over your competition and opening new doors for where your product can be sold.

If your traceability information isn't working to help you buy better, manufacture better, and ship more accurately, those traceability programs will remain just a cost for you. If you are going to track the information anyway, why not get it working for you and use it to increase your profits?

This book is NOT an academic text. It's a practical guide that shares information about traceability and stories from the front lines of plant floors and warehouses of growing small and mid-sized food, meat and beverage manufacturers. These stories and the ideas presented in this guide can help you understand the various kinds of barcodes and how they are used today, as well as the traceability requirements of government inspectors, food safety certification programs, your customers and consumers. It offers ideas on how to achieve traceability using technology, and most importantly, other ways you can use the information gathered to improve and grow your business so you can continue to compete successfully in our growing global marketplace.

# Chapter 2. One-up / One-down, what's involved?

One-up / one-down is a term often used to describe the mandatory internal traceability that government, GFSI certification programs and your customers expect you to have as a manufacturer of food products. Whether you produce for your local market or for worldwide export, this internal traceability is about the information you track within your company, as that is what you are responsible for. One-up / one-down traceability requires the following steps:

1.  Recording of relevant information about incoming goods. This includes the supplier you are receiving from, the shipper who is delivering it, the items, quantities and lot numbers of the received goods, as well as other information, such as certificates of analysis, proving the goods meet any of your required criteria such as organic, kosher, halal, gluten free, etc.
2.  Recording of lot numbers of each raw material used in the batches of interim and finished products you create.
3.  Recording of lot numbers of outgoing goods, so you know which of your customers received which lots of product you shipped.

Hopefully, accomplishing these three steps would allow you, in the event of a food safety concern, to trace a suspect lot number forwards and backwards in your facility. The concern may originate from a customer about one of your finished goods, from a supplier about suspect raw materials, or through discovering a mistake that has taken place in your own facility with a piece of equipment or on a certain day.

In other words, with internal traceability in place, if a finished good was a concern, using the finished good lot number you would be able to determine when that product was made, what raw material lots went into manufacturing it, if you still have any of that suspect lot number of product in stock and what other customers received any of that lot of product. Similarly, if your raw material supplier issued a recall, you would be able to determine if you have any of that lot still in inventory, so you could ensure the remainder isn't used in future production, as well as when you used any of that lot, in which batches of interim or finished goods. Finally, you would know all the customers who received any of the affected finished good lot(s) of product that contained that lot of raw material.

If each manufacturer, distributor and ideally retailer were to do the same and have internal traceability in place, your combined efforts could create an entire history that could trace an item through the supply chain to its original source. That would allow supply chain traceability to be possible. We're not there yet, but many sectors of the food industry are working hard to make this happen.

If your only goal is to ensure you are compliant with one-up and one-down traceability, tracking this information in logs or on paper is currently acceptable in Canada. Many other countries require imported product suppliers to have electronic traceability and Canada is looking at making it mandatory as well. Pulling together the information in a recall situation will often take more time with a manual system, but it is doable.

However, if compliance is your only goal, you may enter into the creation of a traceability system with that one objective in mind— to do what is necessary to satisfy the inspectors. What often results is the creation of silos of information that prevent you from using the information gathered for more productive purposes. By silos, I mean the required information is being gathered, perhaps on paper, in logs or even entered into an isolated program like a

Microsoft Excel spreadsheet, but that the information remains disconnected from relevant, similar or corresponding information gathered in other areas of your plant or warehouse.

To understand the everyday experience of accomplishing one-up / one-down traceability, let's look at options for tracking the information.

To accomplish step one, recording the relevant information about incoming raw ingredients, you could create a paper receiving log for each day. The receiver could record the name of each supplier that delivers that day and each incoming item, the number of units received, the lot numbers for the items received and any other relevant information you want or need to record, such as expiry dates, country of origin, or information you may need to track for satisfying Hazard Analysis and Critical Control Points (HACCP) requirements, such as condition of truck or temperature of the truck.

For step two, recording what the raw material lots were used to create an interim or finished good, you could use batch sheets which would list the required raw ingredients and quantities to pick for a batch. Pickers could record the lot numbers of raw ingredients picked for that batch on the batch sheet including any rework or interim items included. Staff could then assign a lot number to the interim or finished goods created from that batch.

For step three, recording which lots went to which customers, when preparing shipments and picking for customer orders, staff could write down the lot numbers shipped to each customer on the order pick sheet. Those sheets could go back to the office and the information could be copied to send to the customer or keyed onto the invoice or electronic shipping document or logged in an Excel spreadsheet for later reference.

This three-step process would accomplish the minimum requirements of lot tracking. In the event of an actual recall, you would go on a paper trail hunt. Information collected in the above way could lead to a time consuming and painful investigation as the recording above was all done manually and you would have to hope that you could read the writing of those who recorded the information and that they had recorded all that is needed accurately. Because the information exists in silos, and is not being verified, mistakes are very possible.

A given lot of raw material could have found its way into multiple batches of interim or finished product. A given finished good lot could have found its way to any number of customers. When lot numbers are recorded manually, there is no verification that the entry is accurate. If a lot number was incorrectly recorded at receiving, but the pickers of raw materials correctly record the lot number based on human readable information available on the product, your manual records could show that you used a raw material that you never received. Errors are a human inevitability and without some type of verification, like that built into a quality computerized traceability tracking system, they are less likely to be caught.

A manual system also doesn't account well for product loss, whether it is due to theft, spillage, sloppy manufacturing practices or spoilage. Calculating yields from paper systems can be time consuming, and depending on how many ingredients you have in each item, may not be practical. Yet, knowing yields across manufacturing runs is often very valuable business information.

During production and shipping there will always be a percentage of materials and finished products that you will have to accept as losses. It might be that a raw material has expired and this was only discovered when you went to use it. Or, perhaps a given lot of product can't be found when you want to use it. Manual traceability systems don't offer any assistance to help prevent expired product from being used or help you know in advance it is coming due to expiry. This information can help with purchasing, planning production and help ensure accurate inventory control.

The lack of verification in a written system means you can't easily determine what product is missing. While you may know how much you made, if that information is not connected to how much you sold, and similarly if the amount of raw materials you purchased is not connected to how much you used, yields and losses are not easily determined for monitoring.

If you are a distributor, traceability is easier for you than for manufacturers, because distributors don't have the middle step of needing to tie raw materials to the finished goods. For them, the traceability equation is just two steps, recording lots arriving and recording lots shipped. As a distributor however, you are challenged to deal with whatever labels your suppliers provide. You have the tough decision to make as to whether to relabel incoming products or try to use the labels and information provided by your suppliers. Also, if you are a distributor that breaks cases and ships inner packs or individual units, or are a re-packer who kits together different flavours of products creating a new stocking unit, you may as well consider yourself a manufacturer, as you will need to determine a way of tracking what lots are shipped after the product has been unpacked from the cases, especially if the inner units provide only human readable lot information.

Many companies will stop at the point of achieving one-up and one-down internal traceability, even if on paper, once the inspector is appeased. They will breathe a big sigh of relief and move on to other projects. While that is one option, I hope that you will keep reading to learn how you can take that same information you are already collecting and use it to benefit your company in more tangible ways.

# Chapter 3. Barcode Labels for Traceability – How to decode supplier labels

Barcodes are the industry standard method of communicating information in the food and consumer packaged goods industry. They originated in 1974 to help solve the problem of identifying products and prices at checkout counters in grocery stores.

Barcodes are a protocol that can be system agnostic, meaning that they offer a standard format that allows for communication between companies who may be using different software systems to produce and/or read them.

Barcodes are simply a visual representation of a number and/or character sequence. There are different kinds of barcodes, 1D and 2D barcodes are the most common.

Below are images of two linear 1D (one dimensional) barcodes. They are called 1D because they encode the information left to right and traditionally could only be read in one direction, across. Original laser scanners created a red line that would need to be positioned across the barcode to read it. More recently, omnidirectional scanners use a series of lines in varying directions making it easier to pick up all the bars and spaces in these 1D barcodes.

1234567

1234ABC

In 1D barcodes, the more numbers or letters encoded in a barcode the wider it needs to be, to be accurately read by scanners. When barcode scanning technology looks at the bars in a bar code, it simply decodes what it sees into the numbers, letters or characters that make it up. Any sequence of numbers and/or characters can be made into a bar code. Most programs that generate bar codes print the numbers or letters encoded in the bars right below the barcode so it is human readable as well.

## GS1

In order for barcodes to allow for communication between companies, the different companies had to agree upon a standard format for how the barcode would look and what information it would contain. That requirement called for industry collaboration and the organization GS1 was born (Global Standards). GS1 is now a large neutral worldwide non-profit organization. In 2018, they celebrated their 45th anniversary and they describe themselves as the "Global Language of Business" because their standards allow businesses worldwide and across many sectors to benefit from 'talking' with each other using the standardized technology such as barcodes that GS1 has developed. Over 110 countries subscribe to the GS1 standards. www.gs1.org

Businesses use barcodes in two ways. One is for a common communication language between suppliers and customers along their supply chain. The other is for internal use with computer systems for the purposes of managing products within their business. Because bar codes are useful both within and outside a company, you may see multiple bar codes on a label coming from a supplier. The supplier may have included a barcode formatted for internal use, as well as a barcode for use by customers along the supply chain. Sometimes a label may have a separate barcode representing each relevant piece of information (product code, lot number, date of manufacture, etc.) while another barcode may contain multiple pieces of information.

Most inventory scanning warehouse management systems (WMS) use the GS1 barcode standards as the common language that they can understand. This means that the software running on the scanner was programmed to recognise relevant GS1 barcode formats and know how to interpret the information contained to store what is relevant in the correct fields in their database.

**Many barcodes, even certain GS1 barcodes, are not helpful, if your goal is traceability**. If the barcode simply identifies the item, it is useful for inventory control, to ensure you have picked the correct product, but will not help you with traceability.

Most consumers are familiar with UPC codes found on food items in grocery and other retail stores. UPC stands for Universal Product Code and is the North American version of a GS1 GTIN-12. GTIN stands for **Global Trade Identification Number** and is the newer and more widely used term for the unique product identifier given to a retail item.

You can apply to GS1 to become a member and get assigned a company prefix which would form part of all barcodes issued for items you are the brand owner of. You can then assign each product an item number and supply GS1 with information about that item. GS1 organizations around the world operate somewhat independently and some countries have different options for how your product information could get to your retail customers. In Canada, you can add your products to ECCNET, an online item catalogue, then grant other GS1 members, such as your retailer customers, access to the item information you have set up in ECCNET. The retailer would have access to pull this information down from GS1 to their internal system using the Global Data

Synchronization Network (GDSN) to populate their inventory item master.

UPC or GTIN barcodes identify the item and the brand owner, but nothing more, so they are not useful for traceability. (GTIN Info)

**Sample UPC (GTIN-12)**

A GTIN-12 is made up of three sections, the Global Supplier Prefix, the item code and a check digit (totalling 12 digits). The check digit is the final number on a barcode and is often printed in smaller print as shown in the diagram that follows. It is a number that is derived from the other numbers in the barcode and is often used by computer systems to ensure the scan picked up a valid read. A valid check digit simply means that the scanner recognized all the pieces of the barcode.

Note that unless your company subscribes to the GS1 Global Data Synchronization Network (to download GTIN information, which most small and medium sized companies **don't** do), your warehouse management system will only recognize an item if it has been set up in your software's database. Typically, each item you receive or produce gets set up in an inventory system with an item master. If you are using scanning, you would need to set up the GTIN associated with each item so that your software can recognize that item when it is scanned. This is a one-time set up for each item, but a regular part of maintaining a computerized scanning system.

 The GS1 DataBar Omni-directional stacked barcode is a form of 2D barcode that was designed to allow for a GTIN number to fit in a smaller space than a traditional linear 1D barcode could allow. You'll increasingly find these stickers on individual unwrapped fruits and vegetables. It basically stacks the barcode numbers for space saving. It has the advantage of being able to be read in either direction,

Another popular 2D barcode is the QR code which can be found on marketing posters and ads to allow consumers to quickly jump to a website for more information or videos about a product. I will discuss QR codes more in Chapter 14.

To identify the brand owner of any GTIN number, you can visit the GS1 public lookup service website at the link provided below. There you need to type all digits of the GTIN/UPC code including the smaller digit to the left and the check digit to the right.

https://gepir.gs1.org

If the GTIN you enter is not registered with GS1, the barcode could have been made for internal or non-retail use, perhaps representing something the supplier could scan internally to track the product. Or, it could be that the item is from a country where their GS1 organization has not yet linked their internal database to the larger system. Note that it is not a requirement that all your internal item codes be registered with GS1, just those that will be scanned by retailers or distribution partners who get their product information from the GS1 system. Having your barcode number registered ensures that your barcode is unique among other barcodes in your supply chain.

Products that will be sold by retailers need to have an official GTIN on the selling unit. With GTIN-12/UPC consumer codes, the barcode implied unit is one. That is why, if you are buying more than one of an item, grocery store cashiers will either have to scan each identical item individually or scan one of that item and key in the number of units you are buying. Each scan intrinsically represents one unit.

If multiple GTIN units are packed into box and then multiple boxes are packed into a master case, both of those items will also need a unique GTIN number. The box of granola bars would have a GTIN-12 like the individual bar. However, the master case of boxes of granola bars would have a GTIN-14 (14 digits instead of 12).

A GTIN-14 is the typical barcode to identify **trade item groupings** that are not intended for retail sale. GTIN-14 barcodes are found on cases or units that a manufacturer or distributor will sell to their business customers. The contents of a GTIN-14 are shown below:

Picture a box of granola bars you might buy in a grocery store. If the granola bars will be sold to retailers who will open that box and sell individual bars (like a convenience store), the bars themselves would have a GTIN-12 code. Most grocery stores would only sell the box of granola bars (often containing about 6 bars), so that box also needs a GTIN-12 code. Generally, the retailer can't buy just one box of bars from you, but would instead order from you by the case, which would contain several boxes, so that case also needs a unique GTIN-14 code.

That is why for a given item, granola bars, there could be three unique GTIN codes associated with it; one for the bar, one for the box, and one for the case. It has been common practice for cardboard case to be pre-printed with the item code, name and GTIN-14 barcode. Remember, none of the above three barcodes helps us with traceability, they are all designed to identify a supplier, an item and an associated quantity.

GTIN numbers that will flow through major retailers need to be registered with GS1 in the country of manufacture. Retailers, hospitals and other large organizations regularly keep their systems up to date with the information from GS1 about products they purchase, so that they can recognize your item barcodes when they scan them. When a GTIN is scanned, the customers system knows what item it is and whether it is a master case or retail unit based on cross referencing the information GS1 has on file for that code. Note that GTIN-12/UPC codes, even when combined with all the information from the GS1 catalogues such as ECCNET (such as weight, description, dimensions, allergens, etc.), don't tell you or the retailer when that item was made, when it expires or the lot or serial number. Those codes only identify what the item is and static characteristics about the item.

I stress this point because I have often toured food companies where they feel they are ready to implement handheld traceability because so many of their items have barcodes on them. If the majority of their items are only labelled with a GTIN code, unfortunately, scanning won't help them achieve traceability.

Multiple shipping units are often packed onto a skid, which is then called a **logistic unit**. Sometimes a unique skid barcode label is applied to the logistic unit. An SSCC (serial shipping container code) barcode may be part of that skid label. The SSCC is an 18-digit serial numbered GS1 barcode which identifies that logistic unit.

These barcodes can be used internally to manage and move skids around a facility or to offsite storage. They can also be found on skids destined for large retailers or other clients who have the ability to receive detailed information from you, their supplier, about what is on each skid. The retailer would receive the details of what is on each skid from an electronic EDI (Electronic Data Interchange) file called an ASN (Advanced Shipping Notice) that you would send in advance of the shipment arriving at the retailer. For more on EDI, see chapter 4.

**Above is an example of an SSCC (serialized skid) barcode**

This SSCC-18 barcode is useless to a company without the technology to receive the matching EDI file, as on its own, this barcode doesn't identify what items, quantities, lots or anything about what is on that skid. Only when the ASN file is loaded to the retailer's inventory system to populate the inventory with the detailed information you have sent electronically, is there meaning to the scanning of such a serialized label. You can recognize an SSCC code because it starts with the GS1 Application Identifier (00), found in the brackets before the 18 digits begin. We'll talk more about Application Identifiers shortly.

**Barcodes for Traceability**

**The GS1-128 (formerly called the UCC/EAN-128) barcode is the industry standard barcode capable of carrying traceability information**. GS1-128 barcodes can contain multiple pieces or segments of information. If your suppliers label their products with a GS1-128 barcode and you have software that can decode these barcodes, you can capture the GTIN (item) and all other included segments with **a single scan**.

GS1 calls the segment options application identifiers (AI) and most barcode printing programs put those identifiers in brackets right before the contents of that segment. There are more than 100 possible segments to these barcodes. Some are for internal company use and others are for others in the supply chain. These segments are relevant for all industries so many don't relate to food and beverage.

Some examples of AI's you may see on arriving GS1-128 barcodes include a GTIN-14, date of production, weight, date of expiry, country of origin and lot or serial number. Warehouse management systems that can decode GS1-128 barcodes know how to interpret the various segments to store the information needed in the appropriate fields of their database. These barcodes however have a maximum length of 48 characters, including the application identifiers, so you need to choose the most relevant sections to include for your product.

Here is an example of a GS1-128 barcode

(02)12345678901234(10)12345678901234567890(15)090422

The human readable number below the barcode typically puts the application identifiers into brackets to make it easier for you to recognize the different segments and understand the barcode. Barcodes in and of themselves are useless, unless you have a software program that can recognize the format and can decode the information to separate and use the relevant pieces.

Note that not all warehouse management systems will recognize or use all segments. With over 100 GS1 segments or Application Identifiers (AI's) that could be included in any GS1-128 barcode, many warehouse management systems will only recognize and have fields available to store information from the segments most commonly used by their industry. In many situations, WMS programs will simply ignore segments it doesn't recognize, so the barcodes can still be scanned even if they contain extra information you don't need to track.

To decode a GS1-128 barcode, you will need a list of the application identifiers and what they mean. You could then take that list into your warehouse to see what information any GS1-128 barcodes you have on arriving raw ingredients makes available in you scanned them. There is a copy of the GS1 application identifier list at the back of this book. You may want to take a quick peek at the list now to more easily understand the following discussion.

New segments get added as global traders feel the need to track additional information about products. So, if you use this list in your warehouse and see a segment that is not on the list, it could be for one of two reasons. The first reason is that it could have been used for internal purposes by your supplier. You will notice that segments 91-99 are available for companies to use for internal information. Most warehouse systems will simply ignore segments they don't recognize. The second reason an AI might not be on my list is that the AI may be new and might have been added since this book was printed. You can access the most recent listing by visiting the global GS1 website at https://www.GS1.org. Wikipedia also has a list of the GS1 AI's.

Let's take another look at a GS1-128 barcode.

(01)12345678901234(11)131215(10)45678

As the decoder list shows, the (01) application identifier indicates that the number that follows is the GTIN-14 number. Segment (11) is the production date in the form YYMMDD and Segment (10) contains the lot number. Depending on the product there could be additional segments such as the date of expiry, weight or serial number. While GS1 offers an application identifier segment number for lot or batch number (10), you will find some companies put the lot number in the AI segment (21), which is the serial number field.

In the food industry, the serial number segment (21) is particularly applicable to the labelling of catch weight products, which is common in the meat industry. Catch weight means that when that case or item was labelled, the exact weight of that case was 'caught' from the scale and is shown within the label in a segment (310*). When product is tracked by serial number with a corresponding catch weight, no two cases are exactly the same.

For example, you may order a meat product by the case, but are charged by the actual total weight of the specific cases shipped to you. Suppose the standard or average weight of a case of chicken wings is 20 kg, but your supplier tracks the catch weight of each case they produce and sells the wings to you based on a $/kg. In that situation, the actual cases shipped will rarely, if ever, weigh exactly 20 kg. One case might weigh 20.04 kg and another 19.98 kg. Instead of being charged a price per case, you could be charged the $/kg price multiplied by the exact total weight of the cases shipped to you. Such catch weight products will typically arrive labelled with GS1-128 barcodes, which will include a weight segment (310) and a unique serial number segment (21). When such segments are present, it means there is a one to one relationship between that barcode and that particular case.

This is in contrast to lot or batch numbers, where there is typically a one-to-many relationship. A given lot/batch number could be the same for many produced items. If your supplier uses lot numbers, you could receive many units with the same lot number. The same product, chicken wings, could be sold by another supplier as a standard weight item with a lot number. In that situation, the supplier will often quote you a price per case. Of course, that doesn't mean that this supplier's cases were exactly 20kg. It just means that this supplier is not varying your price by the difference above or below the 20kg standard.

If you see a serial number segment (21) on a case, it typically means that no other case exists with that exact serial number--it is unique. There may be multiple cases that happen to weigh 19.98kg in your shipment, but each one would have a unique serial number in the (21) segment. Catch weight serialization is common in the meat and cheese industries.

Sometimes you will find a batch number (10) in the serial number field (21), especially when the label does not contain a segment (10). This is because GS1-128 labels are often produced from a scale station that may be used to weigh both catch weight items and fixed weight items. Some barcode scale programs don't offer multiple label options, so they may just put a lot number in the (21) segment. While this is technically not accurate because a lot number should go into the (10) segment, it is a common occurrence.

A warehouse management system that is capable of traceability will go beyond an inventory system which only tracks items and quantities. It will have fields to store the lot or serial numbers and deal with the other relevant segments you may care about, such as date of production, date of expiry, country of origin or others.

You now have enough knowledge of barcodes to be able to look in your warehouse at what barcodes your suppliers are using. Are they GTIN-14's or are they GS1-128's?

For GS1-128 barcodes you can use the supplied GS1 application identifier list (at the back of this book) to look on the product labels in your warehouse to determine what information your supplier is providing you with now. Remember that there is often information that is printed as human readable on a label that may not be encoded in the barcode. Look at the numbers below the barcode to see what information a scan of that barcode could provide.

Information contained within GS1-128 barcodes, such as lot or serial number is the most important information for effectively implementing a barcode scanning warehouse management system for the dual purposes of inventory control and traceability. If your suppliers are not providing GS1-128 barcodes with a relevant segment for traceability, and you wish to implement scanning for traceability, you will need to relabel arriving products or convince them to apply the required barcode labels before you receive the item.

## How serialized products are recalled by manufacturers

When XL Foods, the second largest beef processing operation in Canada at that time, was involved in a significant meat recall in

Canada in 2012, there were thousands of serialized cases affected that needed to be recalled. Issuing the recall based on those serial numbers would not have been practical and would have made it all the more obvious how many cases were being recalled. So, they issued their recall by the date of production of the product, which was found within the GS1-128 barcode application identifier segment (11).

If you were a customer of XL Foods at the time and didn't have a computerized system that separated and recorded the date of production, it was a particularly painful recall. Many companies with manual systems assign a lot number to incoming product. That lot number is often based on the date they receive the product not on anything from the actual labels from the product. With no link to the date of production, the only option many companies had was to go look at all the cases in stock to determine if any were subject to the recall. It was a challenge for those with manual traceability to determine when they used any affected product and what was made from it and further which of their customers received any of the affected product or any of their own manufactured products that included the recalled product. It would have been much faster to run a recall report to determine this information.

It's important to understand the relevant sections of the GS1-128 used in your vertical of the food industry and to ensure that your information management software system recall reporting was designed to support the ways in which your industry may issue a recall. It will save you so much time in the long run.

TIP

If selecting a computerized system for traceability, ensure that the recall reporting includes the ability to recall by lot number (raw material, interim, and finished good) and by date of production for arriving GS1-128 barcodes, especially if you deal with serialized products.

# Chapter 4. Your Receivers Importance to Traceability Success

Everyone recognizes the saying "Garbage In, Garbage Out" when it comes to computers. If you don't input accurate information, no system will be able to give you accurate useful information back out. A solid traceability system within a company begins with the person who receives the product into your facility. If they get the information wrong, every step that follows based on that information is unfortunately based on error. Below are some of the challenges a receiver can face in ensuring you start your traceability chain off right.

## 1. What should you do when product arrives with labels or documents in different formats from different countries?

Many food manufacturers and distributors import goods from other countries. While GS1 is a global standard in use in over 110 countries, the current reality is that not all your suppliers will follow those standards, so some label formats may be different on goods arriving from other countries. Or, the labels or shipping documents may arrive in a different language or use terminology not common in North America.

Goods arriving may not have the information you need, in a way that it is readily apparent to the receiver or recognizable by your warehouse management scanning system. Your receiver may have to look at the arriving documents or go hunting on the arriving items for the lot number and other relevant information they need to record.

TIP

Carry forward the supplier's lot number, whenever possible. Why? If your supplier recalls their product, they will typically provide the affected lot numbers and/or date of production. Having to cross reference their number(s) against a new one you assigned takes extra time and adds an additional layer for potential errors.

If you walk around your warehouse you will discover that your many suppliers will print their lot numbers, best before or expiry dates and other relevant information in different spots either on the product itself or on labels attached to the product or skid. Your supplier will have used a syntax that makes sense to them or works for their own internal warehouse management system. This format may or may not make it easy for your staff to find and carry forward that information into your system.

Sometimes lot numbers are based on an expiry date or a production date. Some of those dates may be in some format of a Julian date which is generally a five-digit number representing a particular day in a particular year. For example, the Julian date 12621 would represent the 126th day of the year 2021. It is sometimes shown with the date at the front, e.g. 21126. Others lot number formats may be in a form of a calendar date, but because Europeans and North Americans typically write a date differently, even these codes can be difficult to decode properly (130610 could be interpreted Jun 10, 2013 or October 6, 2013 or Jun 13, 2010, depending on the country or company you are in).

If the paperwork that accompanies the shipment doesn't detail the lot numbers, your staff may have to go looking on the arriving cases, bags, pails, totes or drums to find that information. Searching for lot numbers takes time, which slows down the receiving process and therefore costs you money.

Often, you won't want to un-wrap a skid of cased product to search for the lot information on the contained items because you would prefer to put that product away in your warehouse fully wrapped until you need it. That's where it is helpful if your supplier's paperwork provides the required lot information. Remember, however, that everyone makes mistakes; so, if you are going to trust your supplier's paperwork, recognize that sometimes that information may contain errors that you could carry forward if you don't do a physical check.

## 2. Should you relabel arriving product?

One of the benefits of relabeling is that you can ensure all products in your warehouse have a label with a consistent format and appearance, whether it is a barcode label or just a human readable label. With a consistent format, your warehouse staff will have an easier time picking those items for production or picking finished goods for orders, because they will know exactly where to look on the labels for the item and lot information.

To decide if relabeling is right for your company, you need to weigh the benefits against the costs of doing so. If relabeling, receiving staff will require more time to create, print and apply the labels and you will need to provide a computer or tablet, label printer and the accompanying media (the actual labels you print on) near the receiving door. If you don't relabel, it will take more time for your staff to pick raw materials for production. Don't underestimate the time it will take your staff to read multiple label formats and look for the lot information in different spots and in different formats on the various goods in your warehouse. Relabeling the product (by a smart receiver) will also mean that the goods arriving are inspected at the beginning of your process, allowing you to catch mistakes made by your suppliers.

Even if you are able to scan received items, if you are using your supplier's barcodes, you will have to train your staff which barcode to scan for the information you want. That can be complex considering some items will contain multiple barcodes, especially packaging items.

If you aren't relabeling, your staff will need to know where to look on the supplier label to confirm the item code and what number to use for the lot number; sometimes this is not as readily apparent as you might hope. By relabeling with large print easy to read labels, you can prevent staff from having to get off their forklift to look closely at labels and that saves time and money.

Another benefit of relabeling has to do with manufacturing. Your software system often contains recipes (often called a Bill of Materials or BOM in manufacturing) that use a common ingredient item name, such as SALT, but where you purchase SALT from multiple suppliers, each of which have their own item number for the salt they ship you. You could relabel the various arriving supplier shipments of salt, from the various supplier item codes, to a common internally used item code, such as SALT, and record the particular unit of measure and lot number for that arriving shipment. The receiving entry is used to track which supplier that particular lot of salt came from. Your warehouse staff can more easily pick that raw material for production when looking for one common item name in one common format.

If you aren't scanning you may still want to relabel products even with a handwritten tag. You may choose to write your item code, the lot numbers and even the expiry date, nice and big on 8.5" x 11" paper with a permanent marker and put it inside the plastic wrap so forklift drivers can easily read it without dismounting.

If you are planning to scan and products are arriving without a bar code that includes the lot number, you will have to accept that relabeling is going to be a fact of life. I have yet to see a warehouse for a manufacturer where all incoming products were arriving with GS1-128 scannable barcodes—perhaps one day, but not yet. Invariably, there will be goods that arrive with labels that are not traceability scan ready, so you will likely need to invest in a computer station with label printer and labels at your receiving door for managing those incoming items.

The cost and time comparison is a choice between spending more time at receiving vs. more time by warehouse workers when picking product. There is no right answer here and whether to relabel will be an individual choice based on what you find in your own warehouse and what process will result in the fewest errors. Errors in picking and shipping the wrong product can prove costly with fines by retailers, returned product, and unhappy customers, so spending the extra time up front may save your company money in the long run.

## Multiple Languages for the benefit of your staff or your customer

The North American food industry continues to grow more diverse and people from all over the world call this continent home. A variety of companies have been created in order to meet the diverse demands for foods from around the world, and when products are imported, some of the labelling may be in the language of the country of origin. For companies dealing with a variety of suppliers in countries where English is not the first language, you should be sure to check shipments very carefully; it is often helpful to have staff who speak the language of the countries you deal with, so that they can interpret paperwork to ensure you can accurately determine the information you need.

Accuracy in picking products is important, not just to avoid returns, but also to ensure that allergens are treated properly to avoid recall. If you sell to countries where they speak another language, I suggest making the human readable portion of your labels bilingual. A GS1 barcode will be able to be understood in over 110 countries, but the human readable portion of your label, typically consisting of the item name, description, unit of measure, etc. could be printed in multiple languages if that will help increase accuracy within your facility or for your customers. Your foreign customers will appreciate you making it easy for them to do business with you, by using bilingual or multi-lingual labels.

## Where to place the label if you don't want to unwrap the skid

If you don't want to unwrap a skid to label each unit, consider producing a label that represents a single unit that is part of that skid and printing up to four of them (one for each side of the skid so it doesn't matter what way it is placed in a pallet location). If you stick the labels toward the bottom of the skid on the outside of the plastic wrapping, you will have it available to scan or reference while the skid is being unwrapped and units are being picked from that skid.

## 3. How should you receive catch weight serialized product?

Those of you who receive or produce meat, cheese or other food products sold by weight are often familiar with serialized products. Recall that catch weight means that a product is generally priced by weight and you are invoiced for the exact weight of the units that were shipped to you. The total weight delivered to you of a given SKU is often made up of multiple shipping units. For example, you may receive 20 cases of chicken wings with an average case weight of 20kg, so the expected weight of your order would be 400kg (20 cases x 20kg each) but the actual total weight is unlikely ever to be exactly 400kg—generally a bit above or below, such as 401.6kg. Here I outline two methods for managing catch weight product, one without using scanners and the other with scanning.

## The Non-Scanning Method

For those businesses not yet scanning, but who receive serialized product, the best thing to do is to assign each unique product from that receiving a lot number. That lot number will be the one used when you pick that item for further processing or for shipping on orders.

If you have a computerized inventory system you can decide how you want to think of those serialized products moving forward in your own inventory, regardless of how your supplier thinks of that item. It may be that you decide to stock those cases by unit and not worry about the small differences above and below the standard weight of the product. Or, you may want to continue to track that product in your own system by weight, so you can record the total weight and total number of cases arriving.

Inventory systems made for catch weight products in the food industry typically offer the ability to record both the exact weight and number of units for ease of depleting that lot as the product is used or shipped. The total weight and piece count information is generally provided on the shipping manifest that arrives with the shipment. Then, each time you pick from that lot, record the number of units picked, the lot number you picked from and the exact catch weight(s) of the units picked. This will ensure you decrement the appropriate weight from your inventory system.

When assigning lot numbers, it is common to use some format of the date plus a unique number (e.g. 20140815-01, 20140815-02, etc.) Just because your supplier issues serial numbers and exact weights doesn't mean that you have to do so in your system. You may decide to store that product in your own system by unit (e.g.

record you received 25 cases of lot 20140815) and not worry about the small variances in weight from the standard 20kg case weight. Either method is valid; it really depends on the software system you have available, if it has multiple stocking units, what stocking unit you wish to use to track that item in your system and how you plan to invoice your own customers or deplete that item from inventory, to determine the importance to you of tracking the exact weights of those units.

If your recipe calls for using four cases of meat, then whether the case is 19.98 kg or 20.04 kg may not make a material difference for you, so don't complicate your life if the benefit is not there, especially if you don't have an electronic traceability system. If alternatively, your recipe calls for a particular quantity of product by weight, 100 kg for example, you may want to store that item in your inventory system by weight.

If product is serialized and contains a GS1-128 barcode with the serial number and weight and you do have a handheld warehouse management system that can read the provided labels, your receiver will need to scan each case, as each case is labelled with a unique barcode that contains a unique weight and serial number. Scanning each case would require you to unwrap the skid. Sometimes this is challenging if the cases are small and there are internal rows with labels that can't be seen from the outside of the skid. In that situation, you would need to unpack the skid to gain access to all the cases arriving.

There are alternatives to scanning every case however, such as receiving the detailed information about each case and its corresponding weight through an electronic file using EDI (Electronic Data Interchange). EDI allows two companies to exchange information without manual entry. It can work between you and your suppliers or between you and your customers. This electronic information exchange is commonly used if you want to sell your products to major retailers. EDI is another standard communication protocol that allows two companies using different computer programs to communicate with each other.

If you have software that can receive and interpret an EDI document called an ASN (Advanced Shipping Notice), sent to you electronically, you could avoid the step of having to have someone key in detailed information to populate your inventory or avoid having to have staff scan each case. EDI is increasingly being used between trading partners. Most large retailers prefer to place their orders with their suppliers using EDI and want you to invoice them electronically as well. If you have invested in the software to use EDI with your customers, you might want to consider how it could benefit you on your supplier side as well.

**The Scanning Method**

Because catch weight items are all unique, the meat industry and others who sell or receive catch weight products were some of the first companies to embrace handheld scanning. With a warehouse management system that can manage these code 128 serialized barcodes, you can scan the particular cases that are arriving or being shipped and your computer system would store the serial numbers and the corresponding weights to control the inventory. If you have a software program that allows you to ship items by scanning GS1-128 labels that contain the GTIN, weight and serial number, the scanning process of picking to an order makes traceability to each customer at the case level possible and the system should add up the total weight of each item shipped to make invoicing quick and easy.

The type of software that can manage the purchasing, warehouse, and manufacturing aspects and tie it to the orders and shipping and invoicing process is often referred to as ERP software (Enterprise Resource Planning or sometimes called Enterprise software). Wikipedia describes ERP software as "the integrated management of main business processes, often in real-time and mediated by software and technology."

ERP software aims to provide businesses with one core program you can use to operate your entire company tying together the different tasks to allow for overall business management reporting. ERP programs typically include accounting abilities (GL, Accounts Payable, and Accounts Receivable), operational abilities (purchasing, inventory control, manufacturing, product development and QA/QC), customer service abilities (order entry/invoicing) and often offer business intelligence abilities such as report writing, executive dashboards and automated alerts. Some ERP providers will offer fully integrated handheld warehouse management as well.

Some scanning programs don't manage your full business, they are designed more specifically just for warehouse management or for traceability tracking, but the information doesn't flow to invoicing and stops short of providing other business benefits such as cost and yield calculations and overall profitability reporting.

Without a single integrated program, some software vendors will reassure you that it is easy to link their program with another you might be using, with what is called an API. API stands for Application Programming Interface. Wikipedia describes an API as "a set of clearly defined methods of communication among various components." Essentially, software that offers an open API provides a set of instructions for how other another program could interact with the data collected in their program. There is still programming needed following the rules of the API to make the two programs 'talk'. Sometimes that programming has been done for other customers and it is easy for the software vendors to say that their programs integrate.

Please be aware of the limitation of this approach. Generally, only certain limited data is shared between the two systems and from it, you may not be able to easily piece together the overall picture. There are challenges if one program allows editing when the other program does not. For example, you may have a program that can 'send' customer orders to a separate scanning program so that your staff can pick those orders. However, what happens when your customer calls to change their order. Perhaps the order program has the ability to allow you to edit the existing order to add or remove. If the order has already 'gone over' to the scanning program, it's important to know what would happen in the scanning program in that situation. Is it smart enough to know if the order has already been picked and has the ability to alert staff so they don't ship yet? So often I hear stories of companies that chose to implement separate systems that were integrated using an API only to discover that there is very limited connectivity between the two programs and depending on your business, those limitations can make the supposed link relatively useless.

Also, many API links are not live. They may be set to exchange information on a daily or timed basis. If your business has lots of changes close to when you ship an order this can be problematic. Finally, there can be connectivity breakdowns if one of the software programs issues an update adding functionality that breaks the link or requires the other company to program new features or update the information they are sending or receiving between the programs. This is common when using online programs. Often, the developers of those programs are adding new features regularly. The API connectivity to another program will have been designed for the functionality of the two programs at a given point in time. Let's say the program you enter sales orders in adds functionality to allow for change orders. The warehouse program connectivity may have been developed when that feature didn't exist so it is not programmed to allow you to take advantage of it, when it sends the orders over to the warehouse program.

Industry specific ERP programs designed for food manufacturers typically include GS1 barcoding, nutritional panel profiles, EDI abilities, item and lot attribute tracking and most importantly end to end lot or serial control traceability. Other functions that may be offered as part of these food ERP systems is fixed asset management, CRM (customer relationship management) abilities, rebate or over and above marketing program tracking, workflow and sometimes routing (Direct to store deliveries). The common goal of ERP is to help you get rid of silos of information, offer one live program that allows you to collect and use your business information to your advantage.

For reading EDI ASN documents, your ERP system needs to have the ability to load in and interpret EDI documents. For sending EDI documents, your ERP software needs the ability to create the electronic documents for you to send to your partners. If you don't have integrated EDI, you can use a third-party online web service that allows you to key information into it and it creates and sends an EDI version of that information electronically to your customer.

If you are sending and receiving documents directly into your ERP system (no double entry, so less chance for errors) you will need a mailbox service called a VAN (value added network). Essentially, it is a virtual mailbox you use to send and receive electronic mail from your suppliers or customers, called EDI partners. Most major retailers in North America ask suppliers of shelf stable products shipped to their warehouse, to use EDI to transact with them. This consists of the retailer sending their order to you electronically, and you acknowledging receipt of that order electronically and then you sending an invoice to the retailer for the order electronically once you have shipped it. It is easier for the retailer because they themselves are using ERP systems to reduce keying and track costing, etc.

We talked before about other EDI documents such as an ASN (Advanced Shipping Notice). An ASN is an electronic document that gets sent to the retailer prior to your goods arriving at their warehouse. An ASN requires the use of specially formatted skid labels called MH10 labels. The MH10 skid label contains an SSCC barcode (Serial Shipping Container Code as discussed earlier in the book) that is used to match up your shipment with the details of what is on those skids that you sent in the ASN electronic document. The ASN is set up to the specifications of your customer. It would always tell the customer what items and quantities are on each skid. More recently, retailers are asking that the ASN include what lot numbers and/or expiry dates of the items are on each skid. Creating these ASN's manually (without scanning) can be very time consuming as someone needs to write down the items, quantities, lots, and expiries to key them into an EDI system.

When your shipment arrives at the distribution centre (DC) the customer's warehouse staff will scan the SSCC barcode on each skid label and their ERP system will match that serial number up with the contents from the ASN file you issued to them and populate their inventory system with the details of the contents of each arriving skid. It's a great time saver for them, but requires that you have the ability to create EDI documents and print labels in the format required. (See Chapter 12 for more information on EDI)

## Halenda's bingo dabber system

One of the best practical ideas I've come across for those who need to scan in serialized product into an inventory system is what I call 'The bingo dabber system'. You'll need two or three different coloured bingo dabbers for each receiver/picker. Decide on one colour to represent receiving, one to represent picking for production and one to represent scanning for a customer shipment.

The receiver holds the handheld scanner in one hand and the appropriate coloured bingo dabber in the other. Each time they

scan a label, they immediately press the bingo dabber on the case or label. A given skid could have dozens of serialized cases on it and this method allows the receiver to scan while working in a real-world environment.

By that, I mean that in the real world it is rare that a receiver could focus all their attention on one skid for the entire time it would take to scan every case on it.
Coworkers may ask the receiver a question diverting their attention away from scanning. With the bingo dabber system, the receiver can answer the question, and return to their stack of cases and know exactly what case they have already scanned and what they haven't. View a video of this system in use at Halenda's in the blog section of my website Traceabilitymatters.com.

This colour coding system is also helpful for staff walking around the warehouse to know what has been scanned as received, what is allocated for production and what is ready to go out on a shipment. Everyone gets to know the colour system.

This system solves the challenge of staff not being able to keep track of what has been scanned and what hasn't. While the receiver may be able to run a report on their handheld showing what they have scanned as part of a given receiving, the report may just show them a series of serial numbers on a screen that is often smaller than your cell phone screen. It would take time for your receiver to look at the screen and look at the serial numbers listed on the cases to figure out where they left off. Dollar store bingo dabbers are a simple yet effective technique that can save time, especially in a serialized scanning environment.

I've seen how companies with the most successful receiving processes are those who hire a smart and careful receiver. Further, they ensure that the receiver understands the significance of their job to the success of your traceability system.

## Are your distributors covering original manufacturer labels?

Distributors are useful if you want to buy an item but are not a large enough customer for a manufacturer to sell to you directly. Some distributors don't want you to know who the original manufacturer of a product is, so that you won't try to bypass them and attempt to buy direct. To try and hide the manufacturer information, some distributors will put their label directly over top of the manufacturer's label. This is becoming less common as supply chain transparency is being demanded by end consumers and by your customers.

If you find this happening on any items you are receiving, it can cause you problems when it comes to traceability. I have seen this reality when walking around food warehouses. Imagine if you received meat from XL Foods in 2012 but the original manufacturer labels had been covered up. In that case, you may not know the meat was from XL Foods and you wouldn't be able to check your stock against the widely released recall list. Instead, you would have to wait until your distribution supplier issued you a recall using the lot numbers they had applied to the product.

This lost time could pose a food safety issue for your products and your customers. If you find this labeling practice on products in your warehouse, speak to your distribution partner(s) and ask that they avoid covering original labels in future. Your products and brand reputation could depend on it.

Whether you decide to record lot receiving information in a log or use a computer or scanning system to receive your items, all systems are dependent on the information collected (garbage in, garbage out), so pick your receiver carefully.

If you are using a computerized inventory system but not yet scanning, I recommend giving the receiver the responsibility for entering the received goods into the system, rather than having them record lot numbers on paper and sending that paper to the office for entering.

When using two people to accomplish one task, there is no one person whose ultimate responsibility it is to get it right. By giving that responsibility to the receiver, more mistakes can be caught at a time when they can still be fixed and you have one person to talk to when mistakes are discovered.

TIP

> **Hire a smart receiver who understands the importance of the information they collect.**

# Chapter 5. Won't scanning solve all my problems? What a scanning system can't do.

Some people think that scanning is going to solve all their warehouse problems. While I have witnessed the tremendous benefits and efficiency improvements that a scanning warehouse management system (WMS) can offer, it is important to recognize what a scanning system can't do for you. Some business problems are people problems and change management problems and no matter how much technology you throw at those problems, they won't go away without people or process changes. Here are three business problems that scanners can't help you solve:

## 1. A scanner can't recognize product that hasn't been scanned.

For example, if 50 cases arrive on a skid and the receiver only scans 49 cases into inventory, the only way to know one case was missed, is to compare either the quantity ordered to the quantity received or the quantity reported on the receiving documents to the quantity already scanned.

Comparing to the quantity ordered will not be helpful if you order 100 units and your supplier ships you your order in multiple deliveries. In that situation, where the arriving quantity is not expected to match what was ordered, it is unlikely you will catch the mistake. That is why it is important that someone compare the total units scanned to the arriving paperwork piece count as a double check. If those two numbers don't match, someone made an error, either your supplier or your receiver. If you used the bingo dabber system, you could quickly walk around the skid looking at all the cases on that skid for the case that doesn't have a bingo dab on it.

**2. Scanners can't scan labels that have been box cut, were applied incorrectly, are too wrinkled or are otherwise imperfect.**

Have you ever scanned your own items at a self-check-out in a retail store? It can be an exercise in frustration. While scanners are improving, think of what happens at the check-out when an item won't scan? The cashier has to type in the GTIN/UPC code. A consumer GTIN/UPC is typically 8-12 digits, so typing it is doable, but we all know how it slows down your check-out process.

In your warehouse, a traceability ready barcode will be significantly longer than a retail store UPC. That entire number would need to be entered, in the correct order, if the label isn't scan-able. It is a real time- waster when staff members have to type in numbers from barcodes that can't be scanned, for whatever reason.

When you introduce a scanning system, you'll quickly realize the importance of having good clean labels to work with. For this reason, I recommend buying 300 dpi (dots per inch) label printers, as the lines in the bar code will be crisper and have a higher successful scan rate than those printed in 203 dpi. As the label printer dpi goes up, the speed of printing each label goes down slightly; however, with higher dpi you can print small fonts clearly.

Successful scanning and readability are two more reasons to consider relabeling incoming products. While you may have no control over the application or reliability of labels arriving from your suppliers in the short term, let them know if their labels are problematic, as they may not be scanning them themselves and not realize they are applying them carelessly.

The future of barcoding may be in 2D barcodes or RFID (radio frequency ID) tags. Both provide an alternative to traditional 1D barcodes. 2D barcodes are smaller but can hold large amounts of information and only 30% of the barcode (including some key sections) needs to be readable for the scanner to pick up the information (see Chapter 14 for details). You may wish to use a 2D barcode for your internal scanning too. They have a higher read rate yet take up less space on the label. However, I don't see 2D barcodes or RFID gaining mass adoption until the big retailers start using them and demanding them from their suppliers.

For the retailers to adopt these technologies would require many of them to replace their current hardware at their warehouses and potentially their stores, an expensive undertaking. While Walmart does use some RFID reading technology in its warehouses for high ticket items such as appliances, it has not taken off yet in grocery due to the still prohibitive cost of each tag.

### 3. Scanning systems can't help with over or under shipping of lot-controlled items.

Recall that in labels that contain lot/batch numbers (as opposed to serial numbers) you may have many cases that have the identical bar code with that same lot number. To save time, most scanning systems allow you to scan one label and type in the quantity received or shipped. However, if you have sufficient stock on hand of that lot number, say 100 cases of lot 20200815, and you need to ship 80 cases, the system can't know if you actually picked and shipped more or less than the number you input, if you don't scan each unit individually. It can only alert you if the number you say you are shipping exceeds the number on hand in your inventory system.

Some companies solve this by requiring the shipper to scan every case shipped, but again, that takes time and time is money. If you allow your staff to enter the quantity picked, mistakes in actually picking the quantity keyed may happen and this can cause your inventory to be off. This can waste future picker's time if your system suggests the lot to pick based on FIFO (first in, first out) and the system keeps sending your staff member looking for units of a lot that no longer exist, because they were inadvertently shipped on another order or have gone missing.

While it may sound like I am discouraging you from implementing scanning, there is a reason that scanning and warehouse management systems (WMS) are used by most big companies. That reason is that they have been shown to increase accuracy and efficiency and allow important information about what is on hand to be available to those who need it in purchasing, manufacturing planning, and customer service. ERP scanning systems also allow the accounting department to prepare financial statements as the system knows the inventory on hand so they can determine values for that inventory as required.

It is important, however, to recognize what a scanning system can't do for you. That way, you can manage the people issues and train your staff about the limitations of the system and the importance of their attention and accuracy to ensure the entire system works effectively. For example, if a careless warehouse worker doesn't scan product or moves product around warehouse slots without recording it, they affect their fellow workers. They will all jointly have to deal with the consequences and frustrations of sloppy warehouse practices such as product not being where it was supposed to be.

Scanning hardware has come down in price and the options for scanning have increased dramatically in the last decade. The price points are now within reach even for small manufacturers. You can find scanners to work within a wireless network you create within your warehouse, or you can even use cellular scanners if no WIFI network exists. You can scan on the road cellularly and have the information flow live into your system back at the office. You can put wired or wireless scanners linked to mounted tablets on your forklifts.

The main benefit of scanning is the overall increased accuracy in knowing what products are where in your facility and in what products were picked for production or shipped to customers. With the requirements to track more information constantly increasing, scanning could make it easier to the gather multiple pieces of information quickly and to ensure that information flows transparently with minimal effort.

**Should I use lot numbers or serial numbers for my finished goods?**

Below is a flowchart you can use to decide whether you should assign your finished goods lot/batch numbers or serial numbers and whether you should seriously consider scanning or can manage your inventory with paperwork.

You may have some items that the chart suggests you serialize and others where it suggests you use lot/batch numbers. You can treat different items differently in your warehouse.

Remember there are always options. For more ideas, contact me, I am available to help. www.traceabilitymatters.com

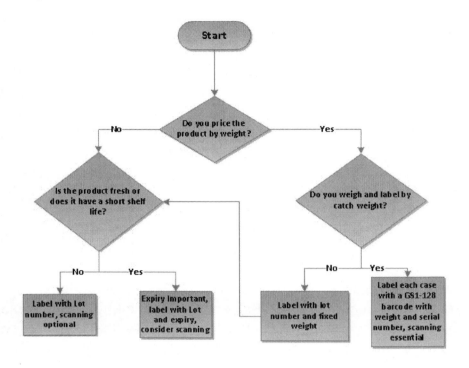

# Chapter 6. Why One-up / One-down Traceability Isn't Enough?

If you have achieved one-up / one-down lot tracking using manual logs you have traceability information, but not necessarily in a way that will allow you to perform mock or actual recalls in any reasonable amount of time. The current time accepted in Canada to provide the Canadian Food Inspection Agency with a distribution list of where all affected product lots ended up is 24 hours (CFIA). However, GFSI programs have tighter time requirements (some are 2-4 hours) and your customers may have expectations of your ability to respond quickly.

For companies using manual systems, 24 hours may not give you enough time to assemble all the required information. While meeting the 24-hour deadline satisfies government requirements, is that fast enough to satisfy your consumers and protect your brand? I have seen manufacturers with traceability software systems provide this distribution list in less than 10 minutes because the pieces required were electronically stored and connected and not in silos. Social media, such as Twitter and Facebook were used by Chobani yogurt customers to share, comment and obtain information about a recall they had in 2013.

Social media provides a platform for consumers to become food safety detectives, posting and sharing information about illnesses to collectively determine a potential source (i.e. What common food did everyone eat?). Once a suspected product is identified as presenting a food safety concern, customers can form an opinion and spread information much faster than 24 hours.

You will be asked to perform regular mock recalls for gaining certification from GFSI food safety programs and you may also have to perform recall audits (or mock recalls) for your inspectors hired by your customers. A great way to test your recall system is to visit a local retailer and buy one of your own products. Bring that product in to your office, set a timer and ask your staff to trace that product back to the raw materials used, let you know if you have any of that lot number still in stock and tell you all the customers who received that lot of product.

If given a finished good to trace when using a written system, this might be a painful exercise. You could do a physical inspection of remaining inventory in the warehouse to see what you have left. You might have to review shipping or invoicing documents to see who else received any of that lot of product. Finally, you might have to go back to the batch sheets from the production of that lot to see the particular lots of raw materials used.

If you have any of lots of those raw materials used still in your facility, and if this was an actual recall, you would want to find them and put those aside on hold and stop using them until you determine if it was an ingredient(s) that caused the problem. Then you would need to look at any interim goods you produced from any of the suspect raw materials.

Those interim goods would go on hold if they are still in the plant. Perhaps you produced a variety of pizzas--pepperoni, deluxe and plain cheese, from the same batch of suspect dough. You would need to trace all those other varieties, including rework used from one to the other, where they went (including any donations and food banks goods) and place them on hold or execute/initiate a recall.

You should also test and time your recall abilities when starting from the other direction using a raw material. When starting from a raw material, you would first determine if you maintained the suppliers' lot number in your facility or not. If you assigned your own lot number, you would need to figure out when you received that product from the supplier to cross reference your logs for what lot number you assigned it internally.

Note that the date a supplier shipped a product to you and the date you received it may be different, if the product took more than one day to reach you. So, if you assign internal lot numbers based on date arriving it might not match a shipment date given to you by your supplier. Once you know the raw material lot you are searching for, determine if you still have any of that lot on hand so you can move the lot into a QC hold area, and then go about determining where you used the remainder.

Be sure to take into consideration losses, waste, product on hold, work in process (WIP), cases of finished product damaged and re-labelled, product sent to company stores and product sent to co-packers (if applicable), or given away as samples or donations.

To do this, you could check the various batch sheets any time after that raw material lot was received to find out when you used the product. If it is a product like a spice, you may have used it in batches for months before finishing that particular lot. In that case, all products which contain that lot of spice would need to be part of the recall. Often products might be produced in stages and production may extend over multiple days.

For pizzas, you may produce the dough first, then perhaps the next day you add the toppings, and cook the pizzas then send them for flash freezing and package them off on the third day. You would have a series of batch sheets and have to hope that you have adequately connected the spice that went into the dough with the pizzas that were made from the dough across the multiple days. Then, you would have to look at shipping or invoicing records to see which customers received any of the finished goods lots that contained that spice. Or, you could just plan to recall everything with that ingredient from the date your supplier issues the recall to now.

The wider your recall the more your brand is affected and the more expensive the recall is to execute. Some people who make fresh products are comfortable with the concept that they will just recall everything from the date of the issue, but for most food companies that would be very expensive and would not be the best strategy.

Sometimes you need to trace product that ran through a particular line or piece of equipment on a day or a series of days of production. This was the case in 2008 when the large Canadian meat processing company Maple Leaf foods had a problem with sliced meat that went through a particular slicing line. If you find yourself in that situation, you may be required to recall everything produced on that date or perhaps just items produced on the affected line.

If you decide to buy a computerized system for tracking lot information, be sure that the system provides reporting that works forward from raw materials through production and out to customer shipments, as well as backwards from finished goods, back through production and to the raw materials that were used to create the problem lot. Finally, be sure that you can also pull up recall information by date of production and/or line if run multiple lines for the same product.

Note that one of the most challenging aspects of traceability is tracking product that is produced over multiple days. Be sure that if any of your products take more than one day to go from raw material to finished good that the system you buy can report recall information across multi-day production. Some examples of multi-day production include:

1) Meat companies who collect trim from their meat cutting room over a few days and then make burgers from that trim. If there was a problem with a finished good produced on either day where trim was collected, all the burgers produced from the combined trim would need to be recalled.
2) Companies that make something one day but package some or all of it the next day.
3) Companies who produce aged/fermented or smoked products (e.g. aged cheese, spirits, breweries, some meats) – product prepared one day may be packed (upon process completion) in several days, months or years due to the packaging form and product type.

I've seen so-called 'traceability systems' that allow you to scan in all received products with the appropriate labels and scan out all finished goods with the appropriate labels, but do nothing to help you record the transformation of the raw materials into your interim or finished goods lots.

Without the middle part of manufacturing, such a system is really just a fancy logging system at receiving and shipping. It replaces the paper log but maintains the silos of information. While such a 'system' may be a good show for your inspections and audits, as it gives the appearance of technology use, a closer look proves that you do not have control of your process and a mistake could ruin multiple production days without you being able to identify the inception and the end.

Logging systems will not show you the movements of goods within your process, the interaction between your processes, the yield and costs by batch and your losses in the process. If you manufacture, traceability is an involved process and any software system you choose needs to reflect and understand your reality.

If one-up / one-down is what you are achieving with your traceability system, depending on your speed of pulling the required pieces together, you will manage to satisfy the requirements of GFSI, your government inspectors and your retail customers; if that is your only goal, logs or simplified 'traceability systems' might meet your needs. Whether one-up/one-down and your speed of responding will satisfy the ultimate consumers of your products, only you can decide. In early 2014, the SQF organization (a GFSI certifying body) announced that they would be the first certifying body to begin conducting unannounced audits. This made many companies nervous that other GFSI bodies will follow suit. Companies who had previously added staff on the days of audits to ensure they could compile required information in a timely way, couldn't do that when they didn't know when an inspector might arrive. Without technology, meeting quick recall requirements on demand may not be possible. This is a sign that speed of assembling information is becoming a requirement that people and paper may not be able to satisfy. Similarly, more and more sectors of the food industry are being asked to contribute to block chains for supply chain traceability (see chapter 13). Having your traceability in an electronic form is becoming a necessity.

What many business owners and management don't always realize is that there are many ways that the very information you are collecting for traceability can be repurposed to offer valuable insights into how your business is operating. Since you are taking the time to collect this information, wouldn't it be great if it could also give you a competitive advantage?

The good news is that tackling traceability in a systematic way can allow you to use the vast data collected to notice trends, to understand and monitor costs and yields, to evaluate warehouse effectiveness allowing you to ultimately make better business decisions.

Let's now turn our attention to the many **benefits beyond recall** that are possible from traceability information and how those benefits can be achieved in your business. This is where you can get a real return on investment (ROI) from investing in technology.

## Chapter 7: Food Safety – catch problem lots before they reach consumers

There are three classes of recalls in Canada based on the likelihood that a product will cause health risk to those who consume it. They are: Class 1 (high risk), Class 2 (moderate risk) and Class 3 (low and no risk).

Within each class there are essentially two kinds of recalls, Health Hazard Alerts and Allergy Alerts. There are those that are the result of an identified food safety concern and those that could pose a health risk to some people due to undeclared allergens or label misinformation. In Canada, for the calendar year of 2018, there were a total of 168 recalls; 54 of those were due to undeclared allergens. That means that 32% of recalls were due to 'allergen' mistakes, which often means incorrect packaging was used, or that purchases/receivers accidentally ordered or accepted raw materials that did not meet your finished good claim requirements. **Invalid source specified.**

This is an important statistic because if you think you are buying gluten free flour and you receive flour and assume it is 'gluten free' and then use to make your gluten free products, it may or may not be possible for your food safety people to catch that. These recalls are often due to operational failings and that highlights an important point—food safety staff in your organization should not be the only ones responsible for recall prevention! Purchasers who deal with and select suppliers, product developers who select and work with new ingredients and suppliers, receivers and warehouse workers who handle and pick raw materials or finished goods for your customer orders and managers who oversee these people are all in a position to contribute to preventing about 35% of recalls, yet many manufacturers only provide traceability and recall training to food safety staff. This might be a big mistake.

When a product is recalled, the brand and company will have to weather a reputational hit in addition having to absorb the financial costs for staff time in conducting the recall and the cost of bringing back or arranging for the safe destruction of your product from customers. Activities you undertake to minimize the need for a recall form part of managing your risk and can make good business sense.

The Grocery Manufacturers Association (GMA) in the US released a study in October 2011 where they surveyed members of their organization about the cost of recalls. While only 8% of respondents were companies with sales under $100M, over 81% of respondents "deem financial risk from recalls as significant to catastrophic". (Grocery Manufacturers Association, Covington & Burling LLP, Ernst and Young LLP) So as you can imagine, for small to mid-sized businesses a 'catastrophic' financial incident could put you out of business or make it hard or impossible for you to find insurance, both recall insurance, if you have it or even commercial general liability insurance.

The same GMA report stated, "Survey respondents generally share the view that recalls have become more common and are likely to increase in frequency and severity going forward." (Grocery Manufacturers Association, Covington & Burling LLP, Ernst and Young LLP) A combination of reasons for this prediction include better technology for detecting food safety problems, for reporting incidences of food poisoning and for tying all the pieces together to identify the source of food safety incidents.

The process of having receiving procedures where the receiver examines the incoming documents and goods for lot or serial numbers, as well as any required additional documents or conditions helps catch problems before you have accepted, put away and potentially used those items in manufacturing. Depending on the finished goods claims you are making, you may require Certificates of Analysis for high risk ingredients such as egg products. You may also need to ensure you have up to date Kosher, Halal or other certifications, as well as allergen or gluten free certificates.

Finally, you may need to confirm the temperature of the truck meets requirements for the products being delivered and that the condition of the truck upon arrival is clean with any seals intact. This can add up to a lot of information. One challenge is how to ensure that your receiver knows which attributes are important for them to check for each raw material they receive. A basic receiving log doesn't typically differentiate the information collected between high and low risk items. This is one increasingly important area where technology can be of value.

Let's return to our pizza making example for ideas on how to communicate these important raw material attributes to the receiver. If you manufacture frozen pizzas, you will be receiving ingredients to make the dough, as well as items such as cheese, vegetables, and meat for the toppings.

There have been very few flour recalls in Canada due to food safety. One, in 2008, was due to the accidental addition of too much fortification ingredients including folic acid, iron, niacin, riboflavin and thiamine. (Government of Canada) Flour is considered a low risk ingredient. For many mid-sized and larger manufacturers, flour is often delivered to a silo. Depending on how often you empty and clean your silo, any problem with flour on one day could affect all future production up to the point that the silo is next emptied and cleaned, if the flour for the most recent shipment is added on top of previous loads and intermixes within the silo.

Your higher risk items are the cheese, vegetables and meat. All of those toppings are in categories where food safety concerns and recalls are more common. Depending on who your customers are and what countries you sell to, you may be required to track different information. If you are a Canadian company but sell products to the US, you will need to conform to FDA FSMA requirements as well as the Canadian Food Inspection Agency (CFIA).

You will want to ensure you track country of origin on some categories of product such as vegetables and you may need to verify that your raw ingredients support any finished goods claims you are making. Perhaps your cheese pizzas are Organic certified. The required raw materials must be certified as organic for you to maintain that claim. In that situation, your receiver needs to check the documents to ensure the raw materials meet your requirements and that any accompanying certifying documents are received as documentation for your claim.

Some companies prefer to receive the items into a hold location for QA/QC staff to review the documents and okay the product for release to general stock. Whether you have the receiver do the check or the QA/QC staff, it is important that you have some type of verification.

One way this can be done is through scanning. If your purchasing staff are careful about ordering only items that meet the finished goods claims and if those items can come labelled with a GS1-128 label with the appropriate segments for traceability, scanning can help ensure you have received the right product and capture the required information at the same time. If your supplier substituted another product for the one ordered (for example, shipped you ten 5kg pails instead of five 10kg pails as ordered) the scan would not recognize the 5kg pail SKU and would not accept the scan until that SKU had been initially set up in your system. That is a perfect time to stop and have purchasing or QA/QC check the new SKU to ensure it meets your requirements. Once they do, and they set up the individual GTIN or SKU numbers in your scanning system, the items can be received and recognized in future should the supplier make the same substitution again.

Another area of importance where scanners can really help is in putting product on hold. One common way to segregate suspect items for inspection is to use virtual warehouses in your scanning system. Often, warehouse management systems have the ability to designate certain 'warehouses' or 'warehouse locations' as being non-sellable. If a user attempts to scan that item to an order, they can be alerted by the software that the product is on hold.

If you need to hold product but don't have the space in your warehouse to create a separated section for storing product that you don't want used in production or sent to customers, you don't have to physically move it, you could instead set up a virtual warehouse location. You might name that location ONHOLD, or QC and transfer product into that location just in the computer. That way, if someone was to try and scan that product to bring it to production or to send it out on a customer order, the handheld would alert them that they can't use that particular lot or skid at this time. If your system sends your staff to the warehouse locations based on FIFO (First in First Out), it can often be set to ignore product in those ONHOLD locations. Segregation is a task that is important in your food safety system and more of a challenge when using disconnected or paper-based systems.

Allergen recalls are often attributable to raw material substitutions. Maybe when you tried to place an order for a specific raw material, your supplier was out of stock and they offered to send you a substitute. It is critical that you ensure all substitutes meet the required attributes of the original raw material (i.e. has the same certifications, allergen profile, etc.). If it doesn't and you order, receive and use that substitute in your products and then discover it wasn't 'certified' Organic, you could find yourself in an allergen/claim recall situation.

Consumers don't necessarily make the distinction between food safety and allergen/claim recalls. To the consumer, a recalled product has a problem and needs to be returned or tossed. This is bad for your brand and could affect consumers future purchasing decisions. Unfortunately, a recall of products similar to yours could also adversely affect consumer confidence about your entire product category, even when your brand was not the one issuing the recall.

In the Grocery Manufacturer's report they tell the story of one US shell egg producer that recalled 500 million eggs due to a salmonella outbreak. The negative media attention produced a drop in egg prices that cost the shell egg industry $100M in September 2010 alone. (Grocery Manufacturers Association, Covington & Burling LLP, Ernst and Young LLP).

Keeping track of what attributes each item is required to conform to, is one excellent example where a traceability system designed for the food industry can be of great use. Such receiving systems often allow for the setup of detailed item master information and entry of receiving attribute information that changes with each shipment (like lot number, expiry date, etc.). If you don't have a system, you could set up a binder at receiving where each item has a page. I have seen manufacturers take digital images of incoming items, highlighting what information to look for on each container/case/bag type, circling where to find the lot number and any other attributes that the receiver needs to check for. If staff can't find the numbers they are looking for quickly, they can reference the binder for details on where to look on that item to find the information.

This can make sense if you buy the same things from the same suppliers over and over. It is less helpful if you regularly shop around, getting raw materials from a variety of suppliers, or if your suppliers regularly substitute or send you the same product in a variety of packaging sizes or containers. Each packaging size or container should have a unique item code, as they are not interchangeable.

As in our example earlier, while you may order five 10kg cases, your supplier may instead ship you ten 5kg cases. Regardless of if you are using a computerized system or a log system; this substitution will slow things down at receiving. When this happens, you want QA/QC, the purchaser or the receiver to stop, slow down and be careful, alerting the required people in the company to confirm this product is okay for your use. This is just another reason to hire a smart receiver!

Assuming you are confident that once inside your facility, you adhere to Good Manufacturing Practices (GMP's) to reduce or eliminate the chances of your processes contaminating the goods you manufacture, your biggest risk comes from your suppliers. All the more reason to choose and approve your suppliers wisely; your product, your brand and potentially your business could depend                        on                        it.

## Chapter 8. Costing benefits – when costs are not what you thought

The food industry is a competitive industry. Many companies I speak with admit that they don't really understand their costs. Perhaps they price their products based on competition or 'what the market will bear'. In that case, a business owner may only examine their costs from an overall company perspective, meaning, they look at whether they are making money across all their products and all their customers.

The process of tracking all the raw materials you receive, what carrier delivered the ingredients and what quantities and lots arrived, combined with the prices you agreed to pay when you placed the order, means that you have the required information to calculate accurate costs for your landed raw materials as soon as they arrive at your dock.

Further, because you are tracking the quantities and lots of all the raw materials that go into making a given batch and the quantity of interim or finished goods produced from that batch, you have all the information needed to calculate accurate interim and finished goods costs, if you have an efficient way to pull that information together.

Accurate costs can be a revelation for a company. When you truly understand your costs, you can make better buying and manufacturing decisions. I have seen companies drop products, product lines and even customers based on learning this more accurate information. You might be producing an interim product that you could actually buy in the marketplace for less than you can make it for, or you might be selling some products at prices that you can't make money on.

Sometimes this will be deliberate. Perhaps you have a 'loss leader' where you sell a product with little or negative profit, in order to gain a customer's business on more profitable items. Or perhaps you choose to make an interim item so you can keep full control over the entire manufacturing process, even if you could buy it for less. If this is the situation, great, those are valid business choices. It is still valuable to monitor what those costs are, so you can make those deliberate decisions based on a full understanding of the situation.

Costing is one area where smaller and mid-sized businesses have a big advantage over larger companies. I have heard that many large companies prefer to use a standard cost system. A standard cost system is just like it sounds. Someone decides a cost for each item and this is the cost that is used to determine inventory valuation and profitability and the cost tracked in the General Ledger (GL) of the company. Standard costs systems are especially popular in industries where the company is publicly traded as it ensures that the financial statements appear more consistent and uniform from month to month.

However, the reality of most businesses is that your costs, especially for food commodity items, do not generally remain the same. Costs may fluctuate weekly or with each new order of a raw material. In addition, landing factors to get the product to your facility such as shipping, fuel surcharges, or other added costs may fluctuate regularly as well. Together these combine to create the real costs that go into determining if your finished goods can be produced and sold profitably. Doesn't it make sense to monitor those costs accurately and regularly so you can adapt as changes in the marketplace happen?

If I've convinced you that reviewing and understanding your costs on a regular basis is valuable, the challenge remains as to how to compile this information in a way that doesn't require you to hire a full-time number cruncher. This is one area where a computerized traceability manufacturing system beats Excel and manual calculations hands down.

Most ERP systems offer a number of costing methods. Recall that ERP or Enterprise Resource Planning systems combine accounting and order entry functionality with inventory and manufacturing abilities. Let's examine some costing options, with examples, for the types of costing that many ERP systems provide. Now before you skip this section of the book because math isn't your favourite subject, I encourage you to keep reading.

It is important for a business owner or manager to have a high level of understanding of how costing works and the costing options you might choose from to calculate costs for your products, because the choice you make (or allow your accounting person to make) will affect the financial statement information you receive from the system about profitability. Since profitability matters to business managers, choosing a costing method to give you the information you expect is an important business decision.

It is my experience that many business owners have been calculating costs since they first started their businesses; they had to! Some did it on paper, others hold this vast amount of information in their heads or use Excel. When implementing a computerized costing system, it is important that the costing calculation best matches how you would choose to cost your products. By gaining a basic, big picture understanding of the options you can ensure that you select the best available method and software program to reflect how you would want to cost those products.

In tackling traceability, you can always add technology and detail as you go along, start by getting the required pieces talking and take it step by step.

TIP

## Options for how to cost your products

I am going to take you through five different costing methods with simple calculations so that you can understand what cost would result using the described method. While reviewing these options, try to determine which method makes most sense for your various items. Some computer systems will allow you to mix and match the methods so that one item could be costed in one way and another item in another way. This gives you the greatest flexibility in ensuring the costs calculated best reflect your wishes and expectations.

**1. Standard cost** – this is a costing method where regardless of what you pay for an item, someone just declares a landed cost for that item and that is the cost that will be recorded in your accounting system for that item whenever it arrives or is used. Of course, the actual cost will typically be different, either because the cost from your supplier varies or the shipping or other extra charges to get the product to you vary. When this happens and a company is using standard cost, all the differences, above and below the standard cost decided are lumped into what is called a 'variance account'.

This is the least helpful costing method for knowing what is truly happening in your company. While it makes sense to establish a standard cost for items if you are, say, projecting sales and costs, it doesn't make sense (in my opinion) to use this as the costing method that is recorded in your general ledger. Why would you want to declare costs and not have them be more reflective of reality? To me the only answer would be if you don't have a system capable of calculating a more realistic cost or if you want the ups and downs related to the realities of buying or the errors in manufacturing to appear less apparent.

**2. Average cost** – this is a rolling average cost and **the most popular costing method used in ERP systems for small to medium sized enterprises** (SMEs). The first delivery of a given item will establish the starting cost. This cost is often made up of the cost of the item plus its share of shipping and any other extra charges to get the product to you.

Let's say that you receive 100 cases of raisins at an average cost of $5/case ($4.85/case plus $0.15/case shipping). That first receipt will establish the cost for that item in the system at $5/case. Perhaps you re-ordered when the stock level dropped to 10 remaining cases, and you then receive 20 new cases of raisins. The system will look at the quantity in stock when new stock arrives and the starting cost to calculate a new average cost. Imagine the cost of each case of raisins increased to $5.20/case on the recent order. The system would look at the overall inventory in stock and calculate the average cost to be:

10 cases x $5.00 = $50 (value of inventory in stock when the new stock arrived)

20 cases x $5.20 = $104 (value of new inventory arriving)

$50 + $104 = $154 (value of all 30 cases in stock)

$154/30 = $5.13/case is the new average cost after the recent shipment arrived

So, the average cost for all 30 cases of raisins would change to $5.13 after the second shipment arrives.

**3. Actual cost by lot** – for actual costing, your system would have to be fully integrated with lot traceability, as actual cost means actual cost by lot. In an actual cost system, whenever a product is used or sold, the actual cost of the particular lot(s) used or sold is recorded as the cost for those items. So, if we use the example above from the average cost calculation, when the original 10 cases in stock were used in production, they would be used at a cost of $5/case. When staff began using the new stock, each new case would be used at an exact cost of $5.20/case. This makes for very accurate costing and many business owners immediately say that actual cost by lot is the costing method they want to use.

Before you decide that actual costing is the best method for you, let me share the disadvantages and the potential unwelcome behaviour that could result from choosing this method.

To illustrate, let's imagine the consequences to interim or finished goods costs when using actual costing. If you made a batch yesterday using the 10 cases at $5/case ($50 total cost for batch A) and another batch today with the cases that had a cost of $5.20/case ($52 total cost for batch B), your two batches would have different costs, even if you used the same amount of raw material and achieved the same yield and quantity of interim or finished goods from the production process. Today's batch is more expensive than yesterdays.

If you only had the overall batch cost information, you might wonder if the staff producing today did something wrong; after all, it cost more to produce that product today than yesterday. Of course, that was not the case.

Similarly, if you can't regularly change the prices you charge your customers to reflect your ever-changing actual costs, your profitability by customer will depend solely on which lots of product that customer was shipped. That could give you the impression that some customers are more or less profitable depending on something that could essentially be considered random, i.e. what lot(s) of product they happened to be shipped.

Further, if you pay commissions or bonuses to your sales staff based on profitability, or margin, they may catch onto the new system quickly and start to ask that certain lots, perhaps not the oldest lots, but instead the least expensive, be shipped to their customers. Doing so could make those customers appear more profitable but not be the best choice for cycling your inventory on first in first out (FIFO) basis. These examples show that it is important to think ahead and talk to your software provider when choosing a costing method to determine the effect your decision may have on reports or employee actions. For industries where the raw material cost varies dramatically with each shipment, it might still be the best approach.

**4. Average cost for an item by location** – sometimes, you will use outside storage or maintain multiple manufacturing and shipping locations. For example, you may have a Toronto warehouse at your manufacturing facility and a Montreal warehouse for shipping to customers east of Ontario. In this situation, you may wish to increase the cost of a given lot of product in the Montreal warehouse to reflect the cost of shipping that product from the manufacturing facility to Montreal. It is important to understand the effect of a costing method choice when traceability is involved when running multiple locations.

If you want to have some of a lot of product available in multiple locations with different costs, be sure that your software supports that requirement. With average cost by location, the average cost calculation would the same as described in Example 1, except the calculation would be done with each receiving at a given location, based on the existing stock and cost of the arriving stock in that location. The reason that average costing, whether it is over the entire company or average by location, is the most popular is because it smooths out any variations in costs so you can better identify trends for your manufactured items without the cost jumping up and down indiscriminately.

Let's return to our raisin example to illustrate.

If we receive 20 cases of raisins in our Toronto warehouse at $5.00 per case with a lot number of 1234, the cost of those raisins in Toronto will be:

20 cases x $5.00 = $100 (in Toronto)

If we ship 5 cases of those raisins of lot 1234 to our Montreal warehouse and want to add some shipping costs for doing so, the cost of the raisins lot 1234 in Montreal could be:

$5.00 Toronto cost + $0.50 shipping/case = $5.50/case (in Montreal)

5 cases x $5.50/case = $27.50 total (value of lot 1234 in Montreal)

15 cases x $5/case = $75 total (value of remainder of lot 1234 in Toronto)

**5. Lot average costing** – sometimes, a supplier may ship multiple shipments of product all from the same lot. Perhaps these shipments are several days, weeks or months apart and the price you are paying for the item may have changed between the shipments. Many ERP systems will not allow you to receive more of a lot of product on a new day at a new price without changing the lot number. You could add a suffix to the lot number to accommodate this limitation or if your ERP system allows for lot average costs, it could calculate a moving average cost for a given lot in a given location.

To illustrate, let's return to the raisins in Montreal.

If we ship another 5 cases of lot 1234 to Montreal but the shipping cost has increased to $0.60/case, the average value of lot 1234 in Montreal, assuming we haven't used or sold any yet, would be:

1st 5 cases = $27.50

2nd 5 cases = $5.60 x 5 cases = $28.00

Total cost of the 10 cases of lot 1234 located in Montreal = $27.50 + $28.00 = $55 or $5.55/case

With this method, the cost in Toronto for lot 1234 is still $5/case, but in Montreal the cost has now changed from $5.50/case to $5.55/case for all 10 cases of raisins of the same lot.

Some systems will allow you to choose a costing method by item, while others will require that you choose one costing method across all items. Obviously, having the option to choose a costing method by item gives more flexibility. Some businesses I have worked with have chosen to use average cost for packaging but actual cost by lot for their main, more expensive ingredients, such as meat. Remember that what costing method you choose for arriving raw materials will ultimately affect the calculated cost for your manufactured products.

## Costing your manufactured goods

For manufactured products that are created using an assembly process (combining multiple raw materials together to create a new product); the cost for a batch would be the sum of the costs of the raw materials used to create that batch. Then the unit cost for the items produced would be calculated as the total of the raw material costs, plus any overhead or labour costs you want to add, divided by the number of units produced in that batch.

Let's look at an example to illustrate. Let's say you produce frozen pizzas. The first step in producing these is making the pizza crusts. Below is a calculation for projecting the cost of a batch of pizza dough. We've simplified it to only include the supplier cost of the ingredients not adding extra costs at this time. The expected yield is 1000 pizza dough balls, not including labour. You can see that the expected total batch cost is the sum of the individual ingredient costs, using whatever landed costs you have chosen for the raw materials.

### Pizza Dough Recipe Cost Calculation

| Ingredients | Batch Qty | Unit of Measure | Supplier Cost | Supplier Bag size | Supplier Pricing unit | Cost per stocking unit | Stocking Unit | Expected Batch Cost |
|---|---|---|---|---|---|---|---|---|
| flour | 100 | kg | $ 7.12 | 25 | kg | $ 0.28 | per kg | $ 28.48 |
| salt | 2 | kg | $ 3.72 | 11.3 | kg | $ 0.33 | per kg | $ 0.66 |
| yeast | 0.5 | kg | $ 6.00 | 0.95 | kg | $ 6.32 | per kg | $ 3.16 |
| egg yolk | 3 | kg | $ 225.00 | 22 | kg | $ 10.23 | per kg | $ 30.68 |
| water | 60 | L | $ 1.63 | 1000 | litres | $ 0.0016 | per litre | $ 0.10 |
| | | | | | | | | $ 63.08 /batch |
| | | | | | | | | |
| Typical yield | | 1000 | pizza dough balls | | | | | $ 0.0631 cost /ball |
| | | | | | | | | |
| Actual yield | | 950 | pizza dough balls | | | | | $ 0.066 cost /ball |

So, the actual unit cost on a day to day basis for a given batch is the **actual** cost of that run based on the input costs fed into the formula divided by the number of units produced in that batch. If those input costs are calculated as standard costs, the unit cost of the finished good will only vary by the quantity of the finished good produced in each batch.

If you had a bad day in production and used the expected inputs but only got 950 pizza dough balls out, your actual batch and unit cost would be higher, as the example shows. Instead of each ball of dough costing 6.3 cents per ball, it cost 6.6 cents.

If each of the input costs are a closer representation of the actual cost for each ingredient, either by being an average cost, an average by location, an average by lot or truly being an actual by lot, the finished good cost is more realistic. As mentioned, if your system allows you the flexibility to set the costing method differently for different items, you might decide to use actual cost by lot for your most expensive or cost fluctuating ingredients in a product, but use average cost for packaging, labels, and other less expensive or price stable raw materials.

In either case, if your supplier increases the cost of a raw material the expected batch cost goes up, even if you use the same input quantities and get the expected output quantities from your batch. For example, if the price of dried egg yolk increases by $10/22kg bag, the new expected cost would be $64.44/batch.

Pizza Dough Recipe Cost Calculation

| Ingredients | Batch Qty | UofM | Supplier Cost | Supplier Bag size | Supplier Pricing unit | Cost per stocking unit | Stocking Unit | Expected Batch Cost | |
|---|---|---|---|---|---|---|---|---|---|
| flour | 100 | kg | $ 7.12 | 25 kg | | $ 0.28 | per kg | $ 28.48 | |
| salt | 2 | kg | $ 3.72 | 11.3 kg | | $ 0.33 | per kg | $ 0.66 | |
| yeast | 0.5 | kg | $ 6.00 | 0.95 kg | | $ 6.32 | per kg | $ 3.16 | |
| egg yolk | 3 | kg | $ 235.00 | 22 kg | | $ 10.68 | per kg | $ 32.05 | |
| water | 60 | L | $ 1.63 | 1000 litres | | $ 0.0016 | per litre | $ 0.10 | |
| | | | | | | | | $ 64.44 | /batch |
| | | | | | | | | | |
| Typical yield | 1000 | pizza dough balls | | | | | | $ 0.0644 | cost /ball |
| | | | | | | | | | |
| Actual yield | 950 | pizza dough balls | | | | | | $ 0.068 | cost /ball |

You can see from these examples that there are many options for why the batch cost could change regularly, from changing input costs or changing output quantity, even before other variables such as labour are taken into account.

You don't need to be a cost accountant to decide what the best costing method is for your company. You simply need to understand the differences and the impact your choice will have on reports that you will be using to make business decisions. Then, choose the method that best reflects what you feel is reasonable and work with the information you get for at least a few months. If you decide it isn't the right method, most systems will have a way that you can adjust the costing method to a different type.

## How could understanding your true costs help you manage your business?

The reality is, if you are doing traceability now, you are tracking all the required pieces for better costing. Calculation of the ongoing costs of raw materials and batches is simply a matter of having a tool through which this ever-changing information can be compiled. To do this in Excel would be challenging because the cost of each batch will vary with the particular inputs used and the quantity produced. But these calculations are completely doable with a computerized ERP system that can combine the traceability information of what lots you used in the batch (remembering what those lots cost you when they were received) to compute a cost for each batch. **Better costing becomes a major side benefit you can expect from using the information you are already collecting for the inspector!**

## The challenge of costing and traceability for disassembled products

If you disassemble products instead of just assembling them, costing and traceability is more challenging. However, technology can make it possible.

Disassembly manufacturing (sometimes called multi-output manufacturing) is common in the meat industry as well as in fruit and vegetable processing; but, is also one way of describing many food processing processes where you generate a finished good plus some scrap that may be used as rework. Disassembly happens when one input produces more than one output. For example, a primary meat producer (defined as a meat producer which has a kill floor) takes in whole animals at the beginning of their manufacturing process and turns those into multiple output items that they sell to their customers. Meat processors will generally weigh those animals soon after arrival as many pay the farmers based on weight.

From the input weight, they may ship some hanging product, cut some sides into primal cuts, either assembling hanging trees of primal cuts or shipping large cuts in totes, and often further process primals into cut meat that is packaged into cases and sold by catch weight. These cutting processes produce usable product, trim, and often unusable product that the manufacturer may even have to pay to get rid of. When one input produces multiple outputs, the input cost must be spread across the output items. Costs can't just disappear.

Let's look at an example.

From 1 kg of pork muscle, let's assume the typical yield is

| | |
|---|---|
| 67.2 % | backs |
| 24.6 % | rib ends |
| 4.6 % | fat |
| 97.5 % | Total |

Note that the percentages don't add up to 100%. There is some loss in this cut process. If we tried to use the yield percentages to apportion the input cost, we would have several problems. We'll start our example with 5000 kg of pork muscle that we bought for $2/kg or a total of $10,000.

| Pork Muscle (in kg) | | 5000 kg | $2 / kg | | $10,000.00 |
|---|---|---|---|---|---|
| Outputs | Yield% | Output | | | Cost based on yield % |
| Backs (in kg) | 67.2% | 3,360 kg | $2/kg | | $6,787.20 |
| Fat (in kg) | 4.6% | 231 kg | $2/kg | | $466.62 |
| Pork Rib Ends (kg) | 24.6% | 1,232 kg | $2/kg | | $2,488.64 |
| **Total Output Cost** | **96.5%** | | | | **$9,742.46** |

The first problem in attempting to apportion the output costs based on straight yield alone would be that the input cost and the output cost don't equal each other ($10,000 input and $9,742.46 output). Costs can't disappear in bookkeeping, no matter how much we wish they could. The second problem is that the costs for the output items is based on the percent yield, not on any reasonable representation of their worth.

With cuts of meat, there will always be an established value for what those cuts can be sold for on the open market. You can see from the example why apportioning costs based on weight would make no sense for this business. The cut process yielded 4.6% fat and if that fat was valued at 4.6% of the input cost, we would assign it a cost of $466.62. When in fact, the fat could not likely be sold for that much and you may even have to pay to get rid of it.

While multiplying the amount used x the cost/unit works for assembly manufacturing, the same principle doesn't work well for disassembly or multi output allocation. We need a method that can account for loss in the process and for the fact that different outputs are worth more than others. Therefore, we need to consider other ways of apportioning the input cost among the output items.

There are better ways to apportion costs, but I have learned that there is no one 'right' way of doing so for every company. It is really a business decision as to what method would create the most realistic costs for your items. So, how do small and medium sized enterprises (SME) disassembly manufacturers apportion input costs?

## Two popular disassembly costing methods

While I have seen as many as nine different methods of apportioning the input cost across multiple outputs, the two most popular methods in my experience are:

1. proportionally by the selling price of the finished goods
2. proportionally using a factor method

Allocating the costs across the output items in proportion to their selling price makes a lot of sense. It means that the items you are able to sell at a higher price get a greater share of the input cost, but that the total input cost still equals the output cost, since costs cannot disappear. Let's look at an example to see how this would work.

Email me at judith@traceabilitymatters.com for a copy of the spreadsheets used in creating these examples if you want to see the Excel formulas involved.

Our input is a loin primal of pork. It weighs 40kg and has a cost of $2.81/kg for a total input cost of $112.40. I am going to show two possible ways for calculating costs for the output cuts. The output cuts are loin main muscle, loin buckeye, pork tenderloin, back ribs tail off and ribs – side brisket removed.

To determine a reasonable cost for the outputs from this primal, we will apportion the costs according to the ratio of the relative selling prices of each cut—so the more expensive items get more of the cost.

To do this we multiply the sell price by the weight achieved of each cut to determine our expected sales from selling the cuts.

Using the total of those expected sales we can determine the proportion or ratio each cut is to the total. That ratio is then multiplied by the input cost to determine how much to allocate to that cut. In this example, we apportioned 16.4% of the input cost to the loin main muscle.

For this calculation to be possible the same software would need to know both the prices you plan to sell those items for and the input cost of the loin.

| Input weight of loin primal (kg) | 40 (21% of hot weight) | | | | | |
|---|---|---|---|---|---|---|
| Primal Cost/kg | $2.81 per kg | | | | | |
| Total input cost of primal | $112.40 | | | | | |
| | | Sell Price | Weight achieved of each cut (in kg) | Total Sales Expected | Ratio of each sell price to total | Cost Allocated |
| LOIN-TRIMMED BONE IN | | | | | | |
| LOIN M&M (main muscle) | | $6.00 | 6.8 | $40.80 | 0.164 | $18.46 |
| LOIN- BUCKEYE | | $4.30 | 12.7 | $54.61 | 0.220 | $24.71 |
| PORK TENDERLOIN | | $9.80 | 1.9 | $18.62 | 0.075 | $8.42 |
| RIBS-BACKRIBS TAIL OFF | | $10.50 | 3.8 | $39.90 | 0.161 | $18.05 |
| RIBS-SIDE-BRISKET REMOVED | | $10.50 | 9 | $94.50 | 0.380 | $42.76 |
| Total | | $41.10 | 34.2 | $248.43 | 1.000 | $112.40 |

The second most popular method I have come across is a factor method, where the owner or an experienced manager decides a ratio that each item represents in comparison to the input. For example, a chicken processor might say that a boneless skinless chicken breast is generally worth 1.2 times the cost of a bone-in chicken breast.

This is perhaps the most flexible method as it allows the user to establish the cost factor for each item that is disassembled based on a numbered weighting scale not tied to any perceived sell price. The producer might also change the attribute value depending on special situations or orders. For example, the producer might decide that whenever the dark meat item chicken breast is produced it will get 0.8 times the cost of any white meat chicken breast.

Let's say that a producer has lots of orders for chicken wings leading up to Super Bowl weekend (where wings is a common food to make while watching the big game). Perhaps the regular attribute weightings established for our example is 2 for breasts, 1.5 for legs and 1 for wings. It could be changed to 2, 1.5 and 2 for the week before Super Bowl to place more of the cost on the wings, since they are the primary reason for the disassembly of the chicken and the other items may have to be sold less profitably that week when people are eating lots of wings and less of the other cuts. It is important that the user responsible for adjusting these factors understand the ramifications of their decisions to the cost that is calculated for each item.

To show how it compares to the sell price method, below is a cost calculation based on a cost factor method for our loin primal with the same input of 40kg of primal and the same output weights achieved. You can see that the costs allocated are quite close using the two methods.

| Input weight of loin primal (kg) | 40 (21% of hot weight) | | | | | |
|---|---|---|---|---|---|---|
| Primal Cost/kg | $2.81 per kg | | | | | |
| Total input cost of primal | $112.40 | | | | | |
| | Cost Factor (as determined by meat processor based on experience) | Expected Cost/kg based on factor | Weight achieved of each cut (in kg) | Cost of each cut if just using factors | Cost ratio (ratio of factor cost of each cut against total factor cost) | Cost Allocated |
| LOIN-TRIMMED BONE IN | 1 | | | | | |
| LOIN M&M (main muscle) | 1.4 | $3.93 | 6.8 | $26.75 | 0.162 | $18.20 |
| LOIN- BUCKEYE | 1 | $2.81 | 12.7 | $35.69 | 0.216 | $24.29 |
| PORK TENDERLOIN | 2.4 | $6.74 | 1.9 | $12.81 | 0.078 | $8.72 |
| RIBS-BACKRIBS TAIL OFF | 2.5 | $7.03 | 3.8 | $26.70 | 0.162 | $18.17 |
| RIBS-SIDE-BRISKET REMOVED | 2.5 | $7.03 | 9 | $63.23 | 0.383 | $43.02 |
| Total | 9.8 | $27.54 | 34.2 | $165.17 | 1.000 | $112.40 |

Owners often understand their products better than most others in their business. So, if you are an owner, don't just hand over costing to a bookkeeper or accountant because you worry that it is too complicated. Keep asking questions until you understand the options and make sure that the option being used for your company truly makes sense.

Knowing your costs puts you a step ahead of many businesses that aren't able to capture or manage that kind of information. Remember, for those whose input costs vary regularly, by capturing the costs of each lot and using that information in determining the costs of finished products, you create a flow of live accurate information that you can use to monitor your business for profitability and success.

*"Traceability and product costing go hand in hand."*
Richard Halenda, Owner, Halenda's Meats

### What's feasible for tracking inputs and outputs in a highly variable production environment?

As part of your traceability program, you are already tracking all the inputs you use and all the outputs you create in your manufacturing processes. You may be recording the inputs and outputs for a given production process, such as producing a batch of hams, or you may only find it feasible to record the inputs and outputs for a production day or from a production room in a day.

Recording inputs and outputs by date or perhaps by line or room is often the best that a manufacturer of fresh product made to order can accomplish. Food service processors, who sell to restaurants, for example, often vary what and how much of each product they manufacture based on orders for that day. Another example would be a fresh cake manufacturer who assembles and bakes based on orders, or a fresh meat processor, who cuts and tray packs for restaurants where the orders come in the day before or even the morning they need to be shipped out.

When you produce to order, your goal is to get the orders filled. Generally, you will never be able to produce only exactly what will sell. If you make cakes, you may have a minimum batch size for your recipe and then have to deal with what remains. If you are disassembling product, you will rarely have orders for all by-products of production. You may end up with extra product for which you have no orders; product that either must be sold at a discount or frozen, which generally decreases the value of that product (frozen products often sell for less than fresh).

For example, a fresh meat processor may cut the same inputs differently today than they will tomorrow. Perhaps our processor sells to major grocery and the grocer is advertising skinless boneless chicken breasts at a special price for a few days. In preparing that order, our meat processor will end up making large quantities of skinless boneless chicken breasts resulting in other products such as chicken bones, skin and perhaps trim. The following week they may have more orders for chicken breasts skin on and bone in. The processor will cut the same input a different way each day and week depending on their orders.

In fresh food businesses, restaurants may place orders throughout the morning for afternoon delivery. So, even when the workers start in the morning, they may not know yet exactly what products they will be making that day and what other products will be left at the end of the day to sell. This is a different kind of manufacturing to process manufacturing, where you can plan in advance what products to make and often make in set batch sizes. This make to order manufacturing adds complexity of trying to determine any live cost calculations.

While it may be possible to keep ongoing track of the input costs going to a cut room or process (e.g. I sent 50 chickens in at $2/chicken), it is generally not possible to complete the output disassembly cost calculations until it is known what the final day's production has been. In this situation, it is common for there to be a finishing routine in computerized systems that will look at the inputs to calculate the total input cost (50 chickens x $2 or $100 total) and then look at the outputs created from those chickens to then apportion that input cost to those outputs based on the chosen disassembly costing method.

**Traceability options for disassembly manufacturers**

Beyond costing, the method for tracking lots in a disassembly manufacturing environment can also be a challenge. Since one input could find its way into multiple outputs (one chicken could become part of cases of chicken breast, thighs, wings, and more), the scope of the potential recall will depend on how tightly you can feasibly tie together the inputs and outputs.

In a fast-paced meat cutting environment, where workers are often paid by piecework according to the weight of cut pieces they produce, the incentive to slow the system down for increased tracking is not there. The margins on these commodity type cuts does not allow for much slowing down either. What I have seen these manufacturers do is simply track what goes into a cut room and what comes out of a cut room.

In the meat industry, most finished products are labelled with GS1-128 barcodes so the scales are capturing each SKU labelled, its weight and the serial number assigned to that product. Those intelligent scale systems can often feed that detailed information about each case to a computerized traceability ERP system by integrating the two systems or having the scale send a file to the ERP system on some scheduled basis. Some ERP systems, like Minotaur Software, actually have their own plant floor modules that can create the weighted barcodes and update the inventory in real time.

If the inputs to the cut room are known, either from scanning the inputs if they are in cases and contain a GS1-128 barcode, or from some type of logging system of lot numbers, we have the one side of the traceability equation. Similarly, if the outputs of finished product are known, again by manual keying or reading files from the finished goods scales or tray packing machines, combined with labelling any interim or trim items that were produced that will be added to or used on the next or on subsequent days, we have the outputs for that day. If those two pieces can be married together in a traceability system for that date, you will have the required link for recall purposes.

Admittedly this would mean that in the event of a recall of any of the inputs, all outputs would be subject for recall, because we can't know with any certainty what specific inputs made it into what specific outputs. The consequence of this in a computerized system is that all inputs are married to all outputs and if a problem is found with a case of chicken thighs, all the breasts produced in that cut room would be subject to recall as well.

While this may seem too broad a scope, in reality, the cleaning for a cut facility often takes place overnight, so, if other products were in the same room, possibly cut on the same table as the thighs, it is reasonable that they should be recalled. In the event of a recall from the raw material end, the government inspector would likely have you pull back all production that could have been exposed to the contaminated product on a cut table anyway, so this level of connectivity is usually fine for traceability. Because the connecting of the inputs and outputs is done in a computerized system based on data fed from the plant floor, staff don't have to slow down to make it happen.

TIP

**In tackling traceability, you can always add technology and detail as you go along, start by getting the required pieces talking and take it step by step.**

When product is not produced to order, often scanners are then used at shipping to tie together which cases where shipped to which customers. This forms the final piece needed for one-up / one-down traceability.

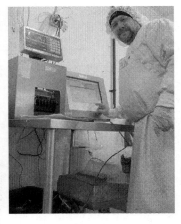

If you manufacture to customer order you could skip the final scanning step by using a weighing and labelling program that allows you to see the customer orders at the weigh station and weigh and label specifically against those orders. In that situation, the software capturing the weight and the weighing and labelling process would typically add that case to the manifest for that customer, so a secondary scan is not necessary.

The above example shows how traceability can be enabled through the background use of technology that can tie the pieces together. The driver for implementing such a system may be traceability, but the business benefit is better, more accurate costing and time savings for staff on the floor and in the office to collect and compile the required information to get an order out the door.

If you don't want to connect the plant floor directly with the traceability system, most intelligent weighing and labelling systems can produce daily summaries of the amount of weight that was scaled off that unit for each SKU on each day. This information could be keyed into a computerized traceability system for the purposes of cost calculations. If you are labelling each case with a unique serial number it is typically not practical to key each of those and their corresponding weights, usually just the total weight and number of units per SKU are entered.

## Multi-Day Production Lot tracking

I can't emphasize enough the importance for traceability of knowing any interim products that remain at the end of any of your production days that will be used, reworked or combined with products on future days.

Trim, for example, could be placed in a metal bin, pushed onto a floor scale to weigh and get assigned a lot number at the end of each day. That interim product lot could become an input into the same or a new process the next day or on a subsequent day.

Only in this way would your computerized system realize that if a problem was found on Day 2 with trim that originated on Day 1 and Day 2, that all of Day 1 products that may have gone into the Day 1 trim must come back as part of that recall.

Be warned, multi-day production is one aspect of traceability that not even all computerized systems do well! If **any** of your processes are not completely finished at the end of each day, make sure you understand how any traceability system you are considering will handle that requirement before you invest in it.

## How yields from traceability helped one meat processor identify and correct a problem with his smoke house

I have worked with many food processors to help them capture and use traceability information. One meat processor who has achieved tremendous growth and success takes traceability and its other benefits very seriously. That company is Halenda's Fine Foods Limited, whose home office and main production facility is in Oshawa, Ontario, Canada and is owned by Richard Halenda. Halenda's produce award winning sausages and also operate a meat distribution business called The Meat Depot and a rapidly expanding series of retail stores focused around selling great local and traceable meat under the retail banner of Halenda's.

Their sausage manufacturing process takes place in four distinct steps. To track the information for traceability as they transform their raw materials into finished sausages, they weigh their products in-between each stage creating interim products that are fully traceable. This weighing process has also allowed them to learn accurate yield and loss information over time so they know what output they can expect to achieve for any given product.

The steps in their process are:

1) Mixing – Creating the filling
2) Casing – stuffing the casings with the mix
3) Smoking – racks with hanging sausages are put into the smoke house overnight
4) Packaging – the smoked sausages are packaged into cases, weighed and labelled

Halenda's uses the Minotaur Business System, an ERP system designed for food and meat manufacturers, where they have set up multiple levels of bills of materials (recipes) for the four stages. When they schedule production to make sausages, their system produces four batch sheets with a unique work order number for each stage to be distributed to staff in each section.

Stage 1: Halenda's use the Minotaur handheld warehouse management system (WMS) to scan raw materials to the stage 1 batch sheet so that the inputs (all the cases of meat, spices, etc.) used in that stage are tracked. When they weigh the completed mix on the floor scale, they input the work order number for that stage (this is because they are using a third-party scale system they had in place and didn't convert to using Minotaur's weigh/label in this situation). Their scale system creates a file that the ERP system reads to deplete the raw materials from stage 1 and create the interim mix for stage 2, assigning it a lot number.

Stage 2: They scan the casings they have picked to the work order for stage 2 and stuff the sausages with the stage 1 mix as another input. When they have their sausages hung on 'sticks' ready for smoking, they roll the entire cart onto the floor scale, tare it based on the number of sticks used in hanging them and enter in the work order number for stage 2 before selecting the weigh button. The scale sends a file to the server which the ERP system reads to deplete the casings and interim mix from inventory and put into inventory the number of kg of cased sausages they are sending into the smoke house.

Stage 3: The product smokes overnight and then is weighed again using the work order number for stage 3, which again sends a file to deplete the cased sausages from inventory and put into inventory the smoked cased sausages.

Stage 4: Finally, they package the product into cases for sale at their own retails stores or for food service sales (restaurants). This involves weighing each case and applying a GS1-128 catch weight serialized label to every case. When production is complete, the detail of all the cases produced, weights and serial numbers assigned are added to finished goods inventory, depleting the previous smoked cased sausages from inventory.

In this way, the entire chain is linked from raw materials used to finished cases produced even though their production took place over multiple days.

You can see that this was achievable even for a company with about 60 employees when they first started. They did need to invest in the software and some hardware as well as absorb some integration costs but the end result is an end to end integrated solution.

As they pick customer orders in their warehouse, they scan the finished good cases against the order pick sheet barcode, which ties in the final required traceability piece, which is, which customer received which finished good lots.

While traceability may have been their goal in installing and implementing the above system, the business benefit was found in having available daily yield and costing information.

Let me share a story of how the yield information helped them identify a problem with their smoke house. It is a perfect illustration of the unanticipated, but very real benefits, that automating traceability can offer to help improve your business.

Halenda's Meats had been enjoying the detailed yield information available from investing in the traceability integration of their plant floor weighing at each of their multiple steps in sausage making. They knew their yields well and their business was growing rapidly. To expand production capacity, they purchased another facility which included a smoke house of the same brand as they had at their main plant. They implemented the same ERP system using similar plant floor scale equipment and began producing a product at the new facility using the same recipe and procedure as their original facility. However, they weren't achieving the same yield. Their yield had dropped. The loss at the smokehouse stage was greater at the new facility than it was at the old.

After first observing workers to ensure it was not a training issue, the owner called in the smokehouse supplier and a visit from a technician determined there was a calibration problem and it was corrected. After the correction, their yield increased to what was expected.

This is just one illustration of how a very real economic benefit, knowing and being able to monitor yields, was achieved through the capture and review of data originally designed to allow for the traceability of the meat through its various stages of production.

What gains could you be achieving by understanding the yields at the steps in your own production process?

# Chapter 9. Profitability reporting – how seeing the big picture can help improve your bottom line?

Profitability reporting is the ability to examine profitability across your business as a whole and across customers and items, to see what customers and what items are your most and least profitable. Perhaps you can make a change to your pricing if your margins are not as you expect and want on a given item, or if you can't change pricing you might decide to drop certain products, lines of products or customers, if the margins you want or need to make are not achievable.

I've worked with many companies who admitted that they did not know how much it cost to make their individual products. They were pricing their products based on competitive products and 'what the market would bear'. By gaining an understanding of their costs, they were able to compare those costs against the prices they were charging their different customers to understand their true margins. They were also able to compare the costs of making their interim goods so that they could decide whether making an interim good was worthwhile.

For example, our pizza manufacturer, with full understanding of the cost of an interim product such as the crust, could decide if making the dough makes sense. If they could purchase dough or prepared crusts from another manufacturer that specializes in that product for less than they can make it, they may reconsider their product line and focus on topping and freezing the pizzas instead.

## The challenge of calculating profits including retailer marketing programs

For manufacturers who sell to major retailers, the prices they charge on the invoice are often not the same as the dollars they receive back when the money arrives. Some customers like large retailers often deduct marketing program costs such as co-op, over and above agreements, 2% flyer contributions, and other fees from the payment they are making. This means that the price per unit minus the cost per unit does not reflect your real profit for those customers. This can make calculating profitability a particular challenge especially if input costs fluctuate and you already operate with a tight margin.

Some ERP systems allow you to set up the various marketing programs so that they are tracked and accrued with each outgoing invoice giving you a better prediction of what the arriving amount will look like and will allow you to include or exclude those marketing program costs when viewing profitability reports. The better handle you have on profitability, the better decisions you can make as to the value of large retail clients.

Many a small to mid-sized manufacturer has regretted becoming too dependent on a single large retailer that might expect price reductions year after year. Most companies I know don't experience cost reductions year after year, so knowing your true margins, though sometimes painful, can be critical to your business growth decisions and success.

**When FIFO isn't enough**

Another complicating factor comes when some retailers, such as Walmart, request a narrower range of shelf life acceptability based on expiry date. For example, you may be asked to only ship product to a given customer that has a minimum of 75% of full shelf life remaining. Even if you have a scanning warehouse management system in place, if your warehouse system default is to suggest product to be picked based on FIFO (first in, first out), the suggested lots may not meet the narrowed criteria of that customer. Rejections or fines are costs that can whittle away at your already tight margin when dealing with the big retailers.

When a customer has a narrower range of acceptability, GS1-128 bar codes which contain the date of production and/or date of expiry can be used to direct staff to pick product that will be acceptable to your customer. For this to happen, you need a warehouse management system that will allow you to set up the customer's 'acceptance criteria' formula and one that has the intelligence to only recommend lots that satisfy the criteria. If you ship product that does not meet their criteria, it may be rejected or accepted and sold at a discount, with you also getting paid at a discount.

Again, keeping track of expiry dates as part of traceability information gathering can help you save money. The examples provided are just some ways for how to make your information work for you and not just think of traceability as a QC paperwork activity. Better business decisions, based on accurate timely information, help you grow your business and manage it for increased success.

## Chapter 10. Food Fraud – proving what you sell is what you claim

Food fraud is increasingly becoming a concern that manufacturers have to be aware of, to ensure they don't unknowingly fall victim. In the Canadian marketplace, it is estimated that food fraud could affect between 5 and 10 percent of products produced. Basically, some unethical people or companies are passing off ingredients that are not pure, not what they claim or not from the country of origin they claim. The biggest food fraud ingredients currently are fish, olive oil, honey, maple syrup and vanilla extract.

In a 2019 study by the University of Guelph (U of G--one of Canada's top agricultural focused universities) found that fish food fraud is a major problem in Canada. "In a new study, U of G researchers found 32 per cent of fish were mislabelled and the number of incorrectly identified samples became compounded as the samples moved through the food system. The findings reveal that mislabelling happens before fish are imported into Canada, as well as throughout the supply chain," said Prof. Robert Hanner, study's lead author. Therefore, this fish fraud likely extends to many other countries as well. Using DNA barcoding the researchers found that "The mislabelling rate was 17.6 per cent at the import stage, 27.3 per cent at processing plants and 38.1 per cent at retailers." (University of Guelph)

If you end up buying and using a fraudulent ingredient in your manufacturing process, your own finished goods claims could be compromised and you could find yourself in a recall situation. Your brand would face a credibility hit and you could be facing a lawsuit if a consumer is harmed by your product as a result. For example, if you use olive oil as a raw material and it was actually cut with another oil such as peanut oil, someone with an allergy to peanuts could buy and consume your product and have a severe reaction. Even if you weren't aware of the fraudulent ingredient, you could be held responsible.

There is an expectation that as a food manufacturer, you will use reasonable means to vet your raw material suppliers to ensure that any claims that they give you are valid. You are, in turn, counting on any distributors you buy from to similarly vet their suppliers. That means it will be important for your purchasers to carefully choose suppliers and for receivers and the QA/QC department to ensure that they receive required certificates of analysis (CofA's), check the information, and monitor that current certificates such as Kosher or Organic are on file and up-to-date and that you are tracking the information needed for each item from each supplier. You may even want to randomly test the raw material on your own or use an outside lab for purity confirmation.

The reality is that a traceability system can't, in and of itself, remove the risk of food fraud. Because fraud is just that, someone along the supply chain passing off one ingredient as something else, it is not something that checking certificates will always catch. If a supplier is prepared to lie about the contents of their product, they would also be prepared to lie on the paperwork. Food fraud is illegal and there have been cases of charges laid and jail time imposed in various countries for these crimes. While a traceability system can help mitigate the risk, through holds or required steps for staff to follow when checking arriving product certificates and attributes, it can't eliminate it.

To help prevent food fraud, the food industry is rapidly moving toward making full supply chain traceability possible. Supply chain traceability should reduce counterfeiting in the industry. We'll talk more about that in the upcoming chapter on Blockchain.

Until supply chain traceability becomes a reality in your vertical sector of the food industry, your company can focus on implementing internal systems that can help you review and compile information about your raw materials and accompanying documents and on choosing your suppliers carefully to reduce your chance of becoming party to food fraud.

.

## Chapter 11. Theft - how traceability can detect and prevent 'loss'

Theft is a reality for many businesses. Food processors often tell me that some of their product 'walks away', especially high value products like meat or smaller, more easily concealed products. Product can disappear and you won't know when or how it happened. Many big retailers that carry drugs, batteries and other high priced but smaller sized items have a separate fenced off area for storing these goods, where they control which trusted staff can go into those areas for picking and putting away.

Theft and the historical practice of 'spiffing' both create particular challenges for traceability. Spiffing is a name given when you give away product, sometimes for less than altruistic reasons, such as to gain favour or perhaps for a better shelf space for your product at a customer. Not that long ago, it was an industry accepted practice to spiff the store manager with extra product, either for their personal use or for them to sell for extra profit.

Knowing what products arrived and what was manufactured and having an inventory system that tracks what has been shipped or used, will help you know how much and what products have gone missing. One benefit of serialized products combined with an inventory control system with traceability is that if cases are scanned in and not scanned out to damaged goods, expired goods or to a customer order, your system will continue to think those cases are in stock. While the serialization means that you could ultimately know what specific cases went missing, generally, you may not discover they are missing unless you go hunting for a particular case or until you do some type of inventory count, which could be as rarely as once per year. However, knowing what serial numbered case is missing won't really tell you if it was stolen or accidentally shipped on an order but not scanned.

Similarly, when product is lot controlled you won't know if product has gone missing or just been accidentally shipped to a customer. With lot- controlled items there can be multiple units with the same exact label. Staff often have the flexibility to key in or override the default quantity of a lot-controlled item, when they would prefer to not scan each label individually. If a picker was supposed to pick 62 cases for an order and accidentally picked 63, yet scanned one label and keyed 62 into the handheld, product would have gone missing. This may not constitute theft, but rather carelessness and your customer may not be eager to let you know that they received more than you said you shipped.

**Should you lot control or serial control your items?**

Whether to use lot numbers or serial numbers is a business decision. Serial numbers are common in businesses like the meat and cheese industry where items may be ordered by case but invoiced by the exact weight of the specific cases shipped to that customer often by a $/kg or $/lb. Lot controlled product is typically ordered and priced by unit. The biggest difference is in how those two items are handled in a computerized inventory system. If each case is a unique serial number and weight, the only way to ship is to scan each case or to produce those cases to a specific customer order when weighing and labelling them. Alternatively, if your cases have the same barcode, your staff would be able to scan one barcode and pick the required number of units. Only you can determine if the over/under weight is significant enough to justify the extra time needed to scan every unit.

One consideration is whether your inventory picking system sends staff to the pick the oldest product first. If product is serialized, it is often not feasible to send staff to go find a given serial number, as those can be up to 18 digits long. It is more feasible to send staff to a particular lot or batch number from a particular warehouse location based on FIFO. If your inventory system says there is product in a particular location or from a particular lot and staff can't find it, it gives you a chance to monitor how much of this loss is taking place and when warranted you could begin investigations to try and determine which of the possibilities, theft or sloppy picking is to blame.

If you are not using racking and binning locations in your warehouse management system, but you are tracking lots and/or serial numbers, your system will only know what product exists in a particular warehouse. To help narrow the search and ensure turnover of inventory in this environment, you could set your warehouse up with active picking locations and overstock locations, where you replenish the active picking locations with product from the overflow locations based on FIFO of date of production or expiry or by date of arrival if you chose to affix a skid label to the receiving. Then with each change over to bring a new skid of a new lot number to the picking location, you could implement a step to ensure staff check that the system says you have fully consumed the previous lot. If the system says there is still some of that lot remaining when there are no cases physically available it will give you an opportunity to try and catch the issues before too long.

With traceability, it is important to know where every case has gone, even if you have given it away. One way to note this for purposes of recall is to produce a shipment for product, even if you choose not to charge the customer for it. This ensures that you have the required information should you need to recall that product.

Knowing how much product you are losing to theft can help you determine how much of a priority you need to place on theft prevention.

## Chapter 12. The Buck Stops Here – traceability to the retailer back door or warehouse

While the idea of farm to fork traceability has been talked about for years, and while specific vertical sections of the food industry have made tremendous strides in these areas, I believe for manufacturers that it will still be some years before it is achieved. We discussed how there are a variety of computer systems for tracking inventory and even a variety of versions of the same program, where depending on the version, the system may or may not have lot traceability functionality included. Or, even if you have a system with the traceability capability, your business may not yet be using that feature. This unfortunate reality is the case even for many large food retailers.

The fancy scanning systems used by many big box stores are excellent at warehousing and inventory control, ensuring they ship the right items to the right stores. However, many of those systems were not designed for traceability. It simply wasn't a piece of information that could be practically tracked when many of them implemented their systems, and unfortunately that is often still the case. Many manufacturers and distributors are not yet providing the GS1-128 barcodes necessary to track lots by scanning, especially across all the categories of food products a retailer purchases. In addition, as retailers expand and acquire distribution centres or smaller chains to bring them under their retail banner, they inherit technology of various abilities and vintages.

Unless the retailer immediately dumps whatever system is in each new warehouse or each retail store they acquire, to implement whatever technology is their current standard, there will be different abilities within a given retailer as to whether they could feasibly accomplish traceability to their own stores, let alone to the cash registers.

As a food processor, you would like to think that your large customers with distribution centres are sophisticated enough to know what stores they shipped your different lots of product to. While they do typically know what of their stores they shipped your product to, they likely don't know what lots of those products they shipped to each store. To do so would require having either consistent technology across their warehouses or at least adoption of a common language that each warehouse could understand. While I suspect that is a goal many are working toward, implementing new technologies takes time and technology transformations don't happen overnight.

This inability to change technology quickly shows the importance of adopting a common language, such as that offered by GS1. EDI (electronic data interchange) can allow for effective communication between partners with different computer systems. As such, adopting the industry language is a good bet for preparing for whatever new requirements might come along.

Loblaw is one food retailer in Canada who requests the MH10 skid label and ASN (advanced shipping notice) EDI electronic document combination from many of its suppliers who ship to their warehouse. This means that when your product arrives at their distribution centre, the MH10 serial number barcode on each of your skid labels is scanned and their inventory system will match that number up with the detail of what you said was on that skid. That detail of what item and lots you placed on each skid was relayed to them by you as an ASN EDI document prior to your goods reaching their dock. With this information, Loblaw is well positioned to track the lots of product they receive in and around their warehouse. However, if they don't ship the full skid to a given store they come up against another lot technology hurdle in trying to track lots to the store level.

Recall that an ASN ties the skid label to the detailed contents on that skid. If the distribution centre must break the pallet into the shipping units, master cases for example, they may lose track of the lot information during that unwrapping and case picking process. That is because many manufacturers are still not putting GS1-128 barcodes with a lot segment on each shipping unit. The lot information will be there in human readable form, but Loblaw is not going to start writing down lots on paper. So, while the retailer may be able to tell you what lots of your products are still in stock in the warehouse, if skid-breaking, they likely are not carrying that detail forward to which stores they shipped the remaining lots of your product to.

When your customers are not carrying forward your hard work in traceability, it is easy to become disillusioned with the value of doing it yourself. After all, when the retailers who deal with the actual consumers of your product won't track the lots to their stores, it opens up any recall to wider geography and increases the manual work that needs to be done should you recall a product shipped to that retailer. The wider the recall, the more it costs you and the higher your risk for brand reputation damage. The retailer may just pull back all of an affected SKU in the event of a recall, at your expense, instead of separating the safe lots of product from the specifically recalled dates or lots. How discouraging!

In all fairness, however, in order for retailers to feasibly be able to track lots to the stores, the industry needs to mature to the point that the majority of items shipped to the retailers contain the lot information in scannable formats.

Some segments of the food industry are further along in the adoption of GS1-128 labels. Most produce and cased meat products have those labels and other sectors are following suit.

Walmart has a 2020 deadline for various produce suppliers to join their blockchain. Doing so will require that those produce suppliers and distributors share information on the origin of their produce along the full supply chain electronically with Walmart. This will be expanded beyond Walmart and beyond produce, so you've taken a good step by reading this book to help you plan to implement traceability technology to automate your lot or serial level inventory tracking.

## The Repack Challenge

There are other traceability challenges, such as repacking, that make it hard to provide retailers with the required lot information for them to consider carrying forward to the store level. I have experienced re-packing first hand and the speed of this process makes tracking a challenge. Retailers work with manufacturers to put products on sale to draw customers into the stores. Anticipating larger than normal demand and to make it easier for store staff, the retailer may request a centre or endcap display which features a variety of your products, multiple flavours and/or complimentary products ready for placement in the stores.

You might work with re-packers to build point of purchase (POP) cardboard displays, and then case break from skids of your products to mix flavours and create eye appealing and centre isle ready skids or half skids, which then becomes a new inventory item. This process often takes space and people power, yet needs to be done cost effectively for the product to achieve the aggressive retail price. I have rarely seen the re-packers tracking what lots of product they use in what finished POP displays. They may know what original inventory skids went into the displays overall, but not which lots of each sku went on each display.

If your product doesn't go directly from you to the manufacturer's warehouse and is altered or repacked along the way, tracking becomes more complicated. If your customer is the end retailer, you will want to ask your re-packer if they can help with the tracking and provide the details back to you. You are ultimately the one responsible for knowing what customers receive which lots of your product should you need to recall product.

Each manufacturer is just one piece in the traceability supply chain path. Until the majority of suppliers of food are able to provide traceability information to retailers in a consistent and reliable way, full supply chain traceability will continue to be a goal, but not a reality. I suspect that as retailers adopt the technology needed to capture and manage this additional information, they will mandate new requirements to supplying manufacturers. So, get ready now while you have time to choose the right technology for your business. By focusing on the many benefits you could achieve in your own business by adopting the available protocols now, you can feel confident you will be ready for those changes when they arrive.

# Chapter 13. Traceability beyond your business – Blockchain and how close are we to achieving supply chain traceability?

One-up and one-down is all about your individual business and tracking what you take in and what you ship out. But achieving internal traceability is part of a much larger movement. The latest push in the industry is to promote collaboration among partners in a supply chain to share information for the betterment of all along the chain. This push is coming from large retailers and food service distributors, essentially your customers. If you sell direct to consumer, there may not be a block chain for you to participate in, at least not yet.

The term Blockchain is everywhere these days and the technology was originally developed to keep track of Bitcoin transactions (a crypto currency). Blockchain has started to become synonymous with supply chain traceability but it's important to understand the role of Blockchain software and software that you might use to run your businesses processes. As Manav Gupta said in his book "Blockchain for Dummies, "To be clear, while blockchain contains transaction data, it's not a replacement for databases, messaging technology, transaction processing or business processes. Instead, the blockchain contains verified proof of transactions." (Gupta)

Essentially, it was designed as a decentralized distributed ledger; a big database that participants in a transaction send and confirm information in and have access to see and/or store at least portions of the chain that pertain to them. Once someone contributes a block to a chain and it is acknowledged as accurate by the next person in the chain, the block becomes unchangeable.

The potential to mine this kind of database for information such as performing a traceability recall quickly is exciting, however, I feel it will still be some years before it becomes a reality across all our food products.

The challenge as I see it, is having each individual food manufacturer truly able to contribute the required information to feed the chain. So many food manufacturers are still doing traceability on paper. To contribute information to make something like a Blockchain recall possible, all the players in the chain need to participate and get the required information into the chain in a timely and sustainable way.

The Blockchain technology itself is not new; it has been around for over a decade. For Bitcoin, a public blockchain, the idea is that each party in a Bitcoin transaction confirms the transaction took place and has a copy of the blockchain showing that transaction took place to prove the bitcoin changed hands. Note that Bitcoins use of blockchain is different than the blockchain that IBM Food Trust and Walmart are implementing. IBM Food Trust is not a public blockchain where you will have full rights to see all information in the chain, it is a private blockchain where you contribute information to and if doing so as part of Walmart's initiative, Walmart would have access to see all the transactions as need be. Whether they allow you to see any more than your supplier and your customer in the chain is up to them.

Food manufacturers may get mandated by their big retail customers to participate in blockchains and that will certainly motivate them to adopt digital traceability. For example, direct suppliers of lettuce, spinach and other greens had a deadline of Sep 30, 2019 to get online and participate in Walmart's blockchain, with other segments of their food suppliers to follow. (Nash)

While traceability is a Canadian government requirement and the ability to perform a recall within 24 hours is a requirement, electronic traceability, while recommended, is not yet mandated, according to my reading of The Safe Foods for Canadians Act. Many manufacturers face even tighter timelines (some report a two-hour deadline) for being able to do a recall by their customers or by various GFSI program auditors. Ultimately it is the consumer that demands fast answers in this information age.

To make a traceability blockchain work, each participating member of the chain would need to contribute their lot information in a timely way after the actual transfer of assets occurs. Realistically this would need to be in an electronic format.

Block chain shows great promise for achieving supply chain traceability in the future, as demonstrated by Walmart's first trial of the system with mangoes, where they were able to trace two mangoes back to the original farmers field in just 2.2 seconds. (Nash) While that is impressive, notice that the product involved (mango fruit) did not change or transform along the supply chain. They also had the farm and all distributors along the distribution network participate in the pilot. Each participant recorded shipping and receiving that lot of mangoes so 'mining' that data for the source was easy. It is not as easy when a product is transformed through manufacturing. While some companies are piloting the use of blockchain in the food industry, I have yet to see the protocols that will be required for manufacturers to participate in such a blockchain.

My understanding of current blockchains for food is that they are requesting what items and lot numbers were shipped to each customer in the chain. The supplier and customer both have access to that portion of the chain to acknowledge that what the supplier said they shipped them, is what they received. For a manufacturer, this could mean sending only information to the chain each time you ship finished goods lots with your customer acknowledging receipt of what you say you shipped. However, that creates a big break in the chain. If all the ingredients are only traceable in the chain to the first point of processing or transformation, the end to end traceability reporting won't be possible. In this model, the raw material chains would end with you and a new chain would begin when your finished goods enter the market, but narrowing what raw materials went into what finished goods would not be included.

That part is internal traceability, the responsibility of the manufacturer and information currently kept within that one company. However, I anticipate new protocols will be developed to make mining your internal database possible, either for mock recall audits or for food safety investigations. Exactly what the standards will be are yet to be determined.

It remains problematic that even food manufacturers who are recording the lots of raw materials electronically, may not be doing so in a software program that validates the information. By validated, I mean using software that has a way of checking to make sure that the transaction is possible and preventing impossible transactions from being recorded. That would involve looking at the information in a live environment to ensure that for each transaction you had enough of that lot, in that location, in stock to make the transaction possible. Using scanners to get this kind of detailed lot information into an electronic system is a good option, but so many raw materials are still not being shipped with the lot information encoded into useful barcodes like code 128 barcodes. That means the manufacturer often doesn't have the information upon arrival to scan many of its ingredients and is left with the job of entering lots into their own system to relabel goods upon arrival, which slows down the receiving process. In a market where margins are slim and competition high, people time is costly, so this is good news for manufacturers.

If companies are using programs like Excel to store their lot information, it's important to remember that Excel isn't a validation program, it is a spreadsheet; Excel allows you to enter any information into a cell. Similarly, many inventory and ERP systems have a field for a lot number, but it is an open field where someone can enter whatever they want. There is good reason for the field to be an open at receiving, because lot numbers can be alphanumeric and the various different suppliers will format their lot numbers in a variety of ways. However, from the point of receiving forward, validation is necessary or true traceability can be lost very quickly.

To illustrate what I mean, let's look at an example. If someone looked at some arriving paperwork and transcribed lot L001 as LOO1 (letter 'O' instead of zero in this example) and they are using a system that allows the user to enter whatever they want into a field, the traceability will break down very quickly. Let's say 10 cases of L001 came into the plant. Without validation, someone may enter a new transaction that says 10 cases of lot LOO1 were used to make something. You end up with a system that thinks you used lot LOO1 (that was never received) and thinks you still have 10 cases still of L001 in stock, when in fact you used them already. In a short amount of time your inventory can become a mess, even though it is in an electronic form. If the system was verifying transactions, as soon as the person tried to enter that they used lot LOO1, the system should tell them that there is no lot LOO1 in stock.

While Blockchains may become relevant to mainstream food manufacturers in 5+ years, the first step is ensuring that you get digital control of the traceability within your own manufacturing organization and get it into a verified electronic form, so you have accurate information available to feed whatever blockchain or blockchains your customers want you to participate in.

Consumers would like, I am sure, to be able to scan a package or QR code on a product in a grocery store and find out where and when it was made and possibly where all the ingredients that went into it came from. A large investment in technology for traceability within manufacturers of food products would need to be made, to make that vision a reality.

But in my opinion, we are far from having accurate end to end digital traceability within many food manufacturing companies. Some have achieved it and others are working hard on it, which is great. However, a vast number of manufacturers are still using paper and unvalidated systems, where the information is not being input on the production floor as it happens, but being input after the fact from paperwork, so the accuracy of the information they have may be questionable and how fast this input occurs varies from company to company. By the time an error is discovered, the goods may have left the plant, making it very hard to figure out what really happened.

Further, it is not clear if there will be multiple blockchains that manufacturers are asked to participate in. For example, will each retailer start their own blockchain or will one organization 'win' and be the blockchain all retailers and suppliers participate in. It also requires buy in from all members in a chain and that buy in won't necessarily be easy to get. Some companies use ingredients from around the world and unless all participants are on the chain a trace back to origin is not really feasible. So many questions remain around blockchains implementation for manufacturers.

My recommendation for individual food manufacturers remains that you work on automating traceability within your own organization so that you can start reaping the benefits of doing so now and are also ready when the request comes to participate in a blockchain.

## Will participating in Blockchain be beneficial for you?

You might wonder how participating in a blockchain could benefit your company and your customers. Below I outline some of the many advantages you could receive from either participating in a blockchain or otherwise sharing information with your suppliers and customers.

## Mitigating or catching food fraud

We discussed food fraud as a growing concern in the food industry. If members of a supply chain were required to share information, you could feel more confident that the ingredients you are using to manufacture your products are pure and from the countries and sources you expect. This helps mitigate your risk as a manufacturer. If you fall victim to food fraud, your customers and brand will be affected, so if gaining better visibility of the chain of ingredients before arriving at your plant helps reduce that risk, it can be a worthwhile business activity.

## Collaboration offers opportunities for mutual improvement

Let's face it, food manufacturing is a tight margin industry and that is unlikely to change. If you can improve your yield, it will translate into greater profits. Working with your suppliers as partners in your success can result in them earning more of your business and can help you grow your business.

Perhaps you buy a commodity type ingredient and sometimes shop around to find the best price and value each time you make a purchase. If you have the ability to track the yields of your manufacturing process when you use the similar raw material from different suppliers, you could have valuable information; information that could help you better compare the different suppliers to determine if the raw materials really are equivalent. These yields could result in a preference for one supplier over another.

If one raw material yields a larger quantity of an interim or finished good than the same raw material from another supplier, the supplier with the higher yield may still offer the best value even if their price is higher. If you shared this discovery with the supplier whose yield was worse, they would have fact-based information to use to try to increase the quality of their product to try to achieve the same yield to better compete. Wouldn't that information be valuable to you if you were the supplier? Similarly, this information could be brought into price negotiations with the various suppliers. If you view your suppliers as partners in ensuring that you produce the best product possible, sharing information about the performance of their product makes sense and could be mutually beneficial. For that, you need data.

## Time savings for you and your customers

Time is money and if you can save yourself and your customers' time, you can keep your prices from escalating and your customers happier.

One way in which collaboration can save time is through the electronic exchange of information and documents. For example, the Canadian grocery giant retailer Loblaw has implemented time saving collaboration using GS1 MH10 labels and the accompanying EDI electronic document called an ASN (Advanced Shipping Notice) for many suppliers that ship to their distribution centre. You may recall our earlier discussion that when Loblaw scans the unique serial number on your logistic unit (skid), the system matches that up with the detailed electronic document.

The ASN document then populates Loblaw's inventory system with the details of the products contained on the skids received, not just SKUs and quantities but also lots and/or expiry dates. This saves Loblaw's time because they don't have to scan all the cases on your skid or have staff key in receiving information manually. This type of electronic exchange of information will continue to become more popular. The EDI standard allows for the exchange of information between supply chain partners, yet allows for each partner to be using their own chosen computer program. In other words, EDI is system agnostic, meaning you don't have to be using SAP like Loblaw is to communicate with them.

One of the challenges from a supplier with the very powerful EDI standard is that it allows each partner (customer) to choose which fields in which order they want to receive the electronic information. There is no industry standard shipping document or invoice. The individual company receiving the document sets the rules for how they want their EDI documents formatted. That means that you can't just have a system make one electronic invoice EDI format, for example. While this allows for you to use the same protocol or standard for communicating with your partners such as third-party warehouses or your suppliers in addition to your customers it means that integration fees or 'onboarding' fees are common when starting to communicate with another company electronically. First your software provider would need to set up the required standard for the company you will be dealing with and then you'll need to test the files and/or labels to ensure that they work before sending your first electronic document to them.

Some partners in a food chain are wary and reluctant to share information. Distributors are often concerned that if their customers know who they purchased their products from, they may bypass them and try to deal with the manufacturer directly. However, if a distributor's only advantage is knowing the identity of the company that manufactured the product, I would suggest they won't be in business for long.

In our world of ever-increasing transparency and with the reach that the internet has provided, sourcing suppliers in other countries has never been easier. With the increased ease of worldwide business transactions, distributors need to fill more value-added roles such as accepting and dealing with the complexities of ordering and importing from other countries, while ensuring they satisfy themselves as to the safety of the food or ingredients they are importing.

Typically the real value proposition of a distributor is that they have relationships in the other country, knowledge of the language, understand the labeling rules, bureaucracy and requirements of both the exporting and importing country and have the ability to buy in larger volumes but sell in smaller volumes to customers that don't want to deal with these hassles. Further, distributors may provide marketing support to the manufacturer which makes the distributor a better option for both the manufacturer and the end buyer to use than establishing a direct relationship.

As mentioned, this same protocol for sharing of electronic documents can take place between your suppliers and you, not just with your customers. If you are scanning every case coming into your facility and instead your supplier could provide an electronic document with the information of what they shipped you, that could be loaded into your inventory system so that you didn't have to scan all those cases, that would save you time and therefore money.

EDI has provided a communication method between partners that is understood by warehouse management systems worldwide. Remember too that EDI can be used with a single company or divisions of a company to send information back and forth, again as a time saving measure to improve efficiencies. For example, some companies have a manufacturing company that is a separate entity than their distribution company. Sometimes this is done for insurance reasons in North America. If you regularly buy and sell between your own two businesses, it could be very time consuming entering detailed shipping information of items and lots in the one company to essentially duplicate that entry as a receiving into the other company. EDI could be used to reduce that administrative burden.

**Co-pack Relationships – a perfect partner to share with**

The perfect relationship for information sharing is between co-packers and their customers. Manufacturers have made the investment in equipment and have the staff experience and knowledge to produce the products they specialize in. Sometimes, they themselves can't sell enough of their own branded products directly to fully use those capital and people resources. Those companies may decide to manufacture products on behalf of other brands to best use their expertise to make money. When manufacturers enter into co-packing agreements with other brands, they become partners in ensuring the best outcome for that brand and would be involved in any recall should any of the products they produced be of issue.

The brand owner may provide everything from the raw materials for the manufactured items, to the cases, packaging and labels to affix to the products. In those situations, the co-packer will be responsible for receiving raw materials from or on behalf of the customer. Then, the co-packer may ship the finished product to the customer's warehouse or may be responsible for shipping directly to the brand owner's customers. When producing on behalf of another company, regular communication is an important thing.

If the brand owner is responsible for ordering and shipping packaging supplies to the co-packer, they will need to monitor the quantity on hand of their supplies at your facility and be triggered to order more when stock gets to critical levels. Co-packers tell me this task alone (how much stock of a given raw material is on hand) often results in a many phone calls, voicemails and emails between co-packers and their customers.

Imagine if your inventory of those particular packaging items could be made available to your customer on a private portal so that they don't have to call you to ask the stock levels. Or perhaps your computerized system could be set up with an alert to automatically email their buyer when the stock level of relevant supplies dips below a threshold. Both of these are possible with business intelligence abilities available in many ERP systems. Similarly, if your supplier could view the quantities you have in stock of their finished products, they could better send you product releases to ship those finished goods to where they want them to go. Emails and phone calls have become an inefficient way to communicate. Web portals or automated communication can save staff at both companies from multiple attempts at trying to reach the other party.

If the brand owner is tracking the inventory and lot numbers at your location in their own system, they will need regular communication from you when stock levels change. This could be done electronically using EDI or via direct file transfers or you could give your customer limited abilities to access the information directly from your ERP system. Your customer may be keeping a mirror of the inventory you have made for them in their own system.

The reality of manufacturing is that even if you plan to make a batch of products, let's say 1,000 cases of cheese, you often won't get exactly 1,000 cases of cheese from each batch. You will follow the recipe and package the resulting product. It may have been a bad day and some product was spilled on the floor and instead of the hoped for 1,000 cases, you end up with 990 cases. Alternatively, it could be a good day and you manage to package off 1,002 cases. Or a mixed day where a forklift drove over some packaging, so instead of using 1,002 cardboard boxes to make the 1,002 cases, you actually used 1,115 cardboard boxes but the normal amount of the other ingredients. These realistic manufacturing scenarios means that the expected raw materials used and the actual consumed differ. This reality is the reason for all the phone calls. "I thought you had enough cases on hand?" your customer questions. "Well, we had some 'wastage' so we actually have less", you reply. This type of conversation is not uncommon. Co-packing relationships make sense but continuous and open communication is a key ingredient for the success of those relationships. So, sharing information between this key partner and yourself is valuable for both of you.

Supply chain traceability will continue to create visibility in the food industry. Farmers and processors of animal products already have to report animal movements to large government databases, in case of disease outbreaks in species. The introduction of IBM Food Trust Blockchain and its adoption by companies like Walmart are driving the further development of supply chain traceability. It is only a matter of time before you'll be expected to be ready to send information about your products to an online database. The exact specifics for manufacturers are not yet clear. We don't have a set protocol or file format that will universally apply to all manufacturers. But the one key thing we do know is that in order to participate practically, you'll need your information in an electronic form. Jump on board to be ready when it does arrive and take advantage of the many benefits you can enjoy in the meantime.

# Chapter 14. The future of traceability—technology and trends that will matter more in the next 10 years

Traceability is not a fad! It is a new reality that will continue to play an increasingly important role in food manufacturing. Technology advances happen daily and with social media, consumers can freely comment on and spread information about your brand and products without your involvement. A good example is what happened in the 2013 with the Chobani yogurt recall. Consumers started tweeting and writing on Facebook talking about concerns that they felt the yogurt may be causing sickness. This type of consumer led information sharing means that customers across large geographic regions can amass their voices and sometimes piece together food safety culprits faster than an inspector can research an individual complaint. Chobani did an excellent job of taking these messages seriously and responding quickly both to ease consumer concern and to pull product from shelves by voluntarily issuing a recall.

I increasingly see information on food manufacturer websites boasting strong traceability practices. Clearly, these manufacturers are proud to inform their customers about how they are accomplishing traceability and many show videos of their production process in the interest of advertising their good manufacturing practices.

Imagine scanning a barcode and being able to see the entire map of where that product has been and how it got to you. I expect this transparency by individual companies will only increase in the coming years and begin to extend across supply chain partners. Here, I discuss some of the technologies in development or already in use to make that possible.

## 2D barcodes

 QR Code  Data Matrix

Both the QR code and the Data Matrix 2D barcode examples above encode the url: www.thetraceabilityfactor.com (the name of my first book). If you scan the QR code with your smart phone, and have a data plan or are connected to WIFI, it should take you right to my website Traceability Matters. QR codes are quite popular for marketing purposes today. They can quickly take consumers to a landing page on the internet where they can read information or watch videos about a product.

2D barcodes were first designed for the automotive industry in Japan but have taken off in popularity for a few reasons. One is their ability to create a more interactive experience with consumers. The QR (quick response) version of 2D barcode has become popular as a way for marketers to get users to specific pages on their websites to dispense more detailed production information. 2D barcodes offer many advantages over the traditional linear or 1D barcodes. They can typically be read more reliably, from greater distances and in either direction, but only with scanners or cameras that have the 2D image decoding capability.

Linear scanners which read a slice of a 1D barcode are not effective for reading 2D barcodes, since 2D barcodes don't contain all of their information in one slice across the barcode, it is contained in separate segments around the square. 2D barcodes can be printed using standard barcode or laser printers and can hold all the segments of a 1D barcode and more, yet take up less space on the label or packaging. In fact, a 2D barcode can hold over 4,000 alphanumeric or over 7,000 numeric only characters. There are several standard 2D barcode formats currently available including Data Matrix, QR, PDF417 and GM (Grid Matrix). Whereas 1D barcodes are limited to English letters and numbers, 2D barcodes can store English letters and numbers plus Chinese characters, voice, pictures and any binary information.

They are also uniquely designed with error correction segments so that if some of the square has been damaged the error correction may 'kick in' and allow the barcode to be read as long as the important pieces called the 'finder pattern' are readable. This requirement for less perfection better matches the reality of production and warehouse environments where labels are not always applied perfectly and where some may be box cut or otherwise damaged.

While 2D barcodes offer many advantages, they will only become the new standard from the top down. If your customers don't have the technology to read them, they won't care if your packaging has them and they may still require that you provide a 1D barcode for them to use. Basically, if the major retailers were to update their warehouse management systems to be able to read 2D barcodes and then request you as their supplier use them on products shipped to them, these barcodes would have the critical mass necessary to catch on industry wide. Until that point, 1D will remain the grocery industry standard. That means that you may wish to use the 2D internally, but might also need to include a 1D GS1-128 or GTIN barcode as well to satisfy your customers or those further along the supply chain.

The new alternative to separate QR and barcodes on an item

In August, 2018, GS1 put a new standard into place to give various carriers like barcodes or RFID tags an ability to point people who take a photo of it to a given website page and also convey various of the GS1 segments that a traditional 1D or 2D GS1-128 barcode might contain. It is called the GS1 Web URI Structure Standard. Its goal is to provide some structure around what format information needs to be presented in, to allow for the information traditionally contained for trade such as lot or serial information to be transmitted alongside marketing type QR website linking. Because retailers still require a GTIN code like a UPC and brand owners had often put QR codes on the same package, there started to be some confusion as to what barcode a scanner should pick up. Therefore, GS1 decided to try and combine these two requirements to make it possible to use just one carrier barcode or tag that could serve the dual purposes. URI in the Web URI Structure stands for Uniform Resource Identifier.

"Web URIs exist at the intersection of these two capabilities; in terms of their syntax, they look like URLs because they specify http or https as their protocol - and they can be configured to behave like URLs in terms of supporting Web requests via the http / https Web protocol. However, they are also a perfectly valid way of assigning a globally unambiguous name for anything, whether in the real world or online" (GS1)

"...from a GS1 DataMatrix symbol carrying element strings, a reference GS1 Web URI can be constructed by simply inserting the actual values of the GTIN, Batch/Lot, Serial Number and Expiry Date into a URI template that looks like:"

https://id.gs1.org/gtin/{gtin}/lot/{lot}/ser/{ser}?exp={exp}

(GS1) In order to make this new syntax gain mass adoption, the various programs that read GS1-128 barcodes will need to be adapted to decode the right information from these specially constructed URLs. I expect we'll see more of these barcodes in the next five years.

## RFID tags (Radio Frequency Identification)

 Like barcodes, RFID tags are a device that can store information—large amounts of information. They are the technology imbedded in most credit cards today allowing you to tap to pay. These cards allow contactless payments, where you simply bring your card in range of a reader without needing to swipe or insert it. While gaining popularity in the retail market, these types of tags have been adopted in limited ways in plants and warehouses. RFID tags are often found in access cards that restrict movement to various areas of a building for security purposes. For major appliances, an RFID tag can often be found on each unit, and with the right scanners, these tags can be read to populate fields in an ERP or WMS system just like a segmented 1D label. In fact, an RFID 'tag' doesn't have to be a tag at all. It can be printed on a sticker from an RFID enabled label printer.

An example in the food industry is the animal ear tag, such as those being used on Canadian cattle. These tags can be read using an RFID wand or fixed scanner where the animal only needs to come into range of to capture the unique serial number contained on the tag and assigned to that number. The numbers assigned to each farmer are recorded when the tags are distributed and this is how they tie the farmer to the tag of the animal. The tags are quite resilient through rain and animal wear and tear.

 Canada was the first country in the world to make it mandatory to tag cattle with RFID tags in 2005. This yellow Zee Tag pictured is an approved tag and shows the

same serial number printed on the tag as would be picked up with an RFID reader (Source: Canadaid.com). That allows kill floors that receive the animals the option to read the tags if they have RFID readers, or to collect and record the serial numbers manually from the human readable numbers if they do not. The tag history from farmer, through transporter and interim owners such as stockyards to kill floor is tracked in a centralized database in Canada should the history be relevant for future food safety concerns or animal disease outbreaks.

RFID tags can store an item identifier similar to a GS1 GTIN number in a 1D or 2D barcode. Such tags could be used to identify an item, a case or a pallet. RFID tags have an antenna that can be read by radio scanners that are either handheld or placed at doorways to allow for all items passing under them to be read automatically. If each case of meat had such a tag and the doors to the facility were monitored for these tags, theft detection would be possible. Door readers could reduce the need for handheld scanners as product movement could be recorded as product travels around and out of a warehouse.

Canadian Animal ear tags are LF (low frequency) RFID tags. RFID tags used in other sectors and even on animals in other countries are now often UHF (ultra high frequency). UHF tags are being tested for use in Canada but the read rate has been less reliable when on a moving animal than LF so they have not been adopted in Canada yet. There are many more hardware reader options for UHF tags including the ability to have networked TCP/IP tag readers for UHF, so hopefully they will be adopted in Canada soon. I haven't seen a single LF animal ear tag reader that is ethernet or able to transmit information to a server without being cord connected and little effort is being put in to develop such readers as the LF tags are on their way out. (Moroz, RFID Canada)

Another of the advantages of RFID tags is that some of them (such as the UHF tags mentioned above) are rewriteable, meaning that information could be added to the tag, not just read from it. This reality makes the RFID tag an interesting option because information could be added to the tag as it travels along a supply chain.

If RFID tags were placed on individual consumer items, a consumer could walk under an RFID reader with their cart and the entire contents of the cart could be recorded by doing so. This could certainly speed up the checkout process.

Currently, it is the cost per tag and the cost to buy the accompanying hardware to read the tags that are the primary reasons this technology has not fully taken off yet in warehouses and for retail food items. Note the many newly purchased scanners have the ability to read 1D, 2D and RFID. The cost of an RFID label is about $0.07 to $0.11 USD each, which is still prohibitive for mainstream use, as that would add to the cost of each food item tagged. (Moroz, President, RFID Canada) Additionally, if your customers further along the supply chain don't adopt the technology to read those tags, they essentially become only valuable for your internal use, so until widespread adoption of these alternatives begins, the barcodes will continue to reign.

**DNA traceability**

Food has DNA just like people. This unique fact sets the stage for discovering the source ingredients especially in meat or other animal products. For example, a company called IdentiGEN offers DNA TraceBack® which makes it possible to trace whole muscle cuts from the grocery store back to the individual animal the meat came from.

It can even work with ground meat to tell you what mix of DNA (or which specific cows) made up the meat tested. Of course, for this to work, the DNA of each cow must be registered, which is not currently a common practice and would add to the cost of producing the meat. If you think this is too theoretical and futuristic you may be interested to know that Loblaw, a leading Canadian grocery retailer, signed an agreement in 2014 to pilot a project with IdentiGEN for verifying their beef products in store. (IdentiGEN)

While it is possible to do this farm to fork traceability now, it is scaling the concept and technology to get enough companies in the chain connected to provide their part of the information that will take time. Having a retail sponsor like Loblaw is a sign that the push to participate will come from the top down—in other words, your large customers will decide what technology they will require their suppliers to have and then begin to demand it and put deadlines on your adoption. Someday we may be able to use a phone app to scan our meat in the retail store and have it display the entire history of the product, what animals it originated from and what processing and steps it went through to arrive in our hands.

The future is coming fast as technology continues to advance quickly making it possible for such large amounts of information to be stored and mined for trends and useful information. The sooner you jump on the bandwagon, the more that information can begin working for you now.

## Nanotechnology Tagging

Another form of 'tagging' for both food fraud and for traceability is the ability to add a unique identifying minute tag as an ingredient in food products and read that tag later in the food chain.

Nanotechnology is defined as the manipulation of matter in the size range of 1 to 100 nanometers (1 nanometer is 1 billionth of a meter).

So while nanotechnology encompasses a broad field of science across industries as defined by size, in the food industry, companies such as TruTag Technologies have created inert, edible, heat resistant, virtually invisible but completely identifiable and unique silica 'barcodes' they call TruTags® which can carry product intelligence such as "batch number, manufacturing date, plant location" country of origin and more.

While these tags must be read with proprietary technology offered by that company, they don't have to be examined in a lab. They are 'field readable' with the custom optical reader offered by the company. They report that over $600 Billion in counterfeit goods are sold worldwide every year. Their technology can be used for everything from purses (think fake Gucci bags) to pharmaceuticals, electronic chips and of course in the food industry where it can be added to packaging or to the powders, oils or food coatings.

**All of the technologies mentioned in this chapter are available now, most have just not been widely adopted yet.** There could even be a new technology that could come along and be so superior to what we are doing now that mass adoption occurs in a very short amount of time. Remember in the early 2000's that there was a battle between Blue Ray and DVD for who would win the consumer video market player category. Blue Ray seemed a better technology with a better picture quality but DVD was cheaper and more widely available so it became the choice for mass adoption. That was in the days when you went to a video store to rent movies to watch at home.

Then along came Netflix making both those technologies unnecessary and inferior options. Netflix was founded in 1997 and they gained mass adoption in a very short time.

**Forced supply chain integration**

Regardless of the technology used to tag or label a given food ingredient or product, it is only a matter of time before all food manufacturers and distributors will be required to participate in information sharing platforms, at least in certain circumstances. Theoretically, every supplier could be required to send all data to a giant central database or blockchain with everything they received, and produced and everywhere they shipped each item. I don't see that happening in the next five years.

Since the goal of government inspectors is to be able to quickly conduct food safety or allergen investigations, in the cases of foodborne illness outbreaks or when an issue has been raised, I think we may see a protocol for information storage with a requirement for you to make available your data in the specific incidences of food safety investigations. Consumers will certainly advocate for this.

Of all organizations, GS1 is well positioned to become the body to manage such a protocol, given that manufacturers who sell their products to retail are already GS1 members. Besides issuing individual supplier prefixes and maintaining a database of your finished product codes and distributing information via their Global Data Synchronization Network (GDSN), GS1 also distributes numbers called the GLN, or Global Location Number. A GLN is a unique code to identify a location where information is gathered or created.

Further, the GS1 EPC program in Europe appears to creating a uniform structure for storing and sharing information about products and traceability for use between trading partners. This would be similar to EDI that you might do for receiving orders from and billing your large retail customers. An industry standard would be valuable so that software companies could adopt the standard and ensure that documents arriving and leaving their systems could be easily read by partners with different systems.

With GS1 location identification, standard protocols being increasingly adopted and more companies capable of electronic information exchange, it is becoming more possible to consider tracing supply chain histories. GS1 appear to have many of the required pieces in place already to potentially expand their scope to gathering entire 'trip' information about products. But IBM also has first mover advantage and clout by partnering with Walmart on their Food Trust Blockchain.

There are several other collectives of companies, industry associations and regional groups that are piloting traceability technology like information centralization and sharing, like IBM Food Trust, to help build the business case for such collaborations.

I do believe that an ability to assemble, quickly and consistently, the travel path of ingredients from farm to retailer and eventually to consumer, is coming; it is just a matter of how it will be accomplished and how long it takes to be adopted.

The Institute of Food Technologists (IFT), another non-profit organization who recognized the importance of traceability, has been working through the possibilities in the past few years. In 2013, they launched the Global Food Traceability Center with the mandate to "serve as an authoritative, scientific, and unbiased source for food traceability." The GFTC mission includes traceability "Protocols and Standards, Technology Transfer,

Education and Training and Research". They recognize the value of having the ability to bring together the information pieces within food supply chains. However, they didn't feel a central database of all information was feasible. Instead they pictured a common storage protocol being adopted so that different suppliers of technology could agree to store pertinent lot information in a way that could be queried by an outside system as required. In this model, you would be required to adopt a compatible electronic system and if any of your products or ingredients became suspect in a foodborne outbreak, you would agree to allow the government or other relevant body access to the information. (Institute of Food Technologists)

What all this means for manufacturers is that sooner or later you will be required to maintain lot or serial information **electronically**, so that it can be accessed as required, either mandated by government or by your customers such as retailers or food service distributors.

Gone are the days of quietly spiffing a grocery manager with some free product on the side. Traceability requires you to account for all products you produce. While you can still give away product without charging a customer, you have to record where you sent it for potential recall.

Supply chain traceability is further ahead in some sectors. For example, due to the importance that pharmaceutical drugs play in consumers lives, we expect that a given medicine really contains the right ingredients in the right quantities. Traceability is widely accepted in that industry. Based on recent deadlines, you can pretty much expect that every single blister packed prescription pill is serialized and there are deadlines in place for manufacturers and distributors to get on board with a program called APCIS, which requires them to be able to track the serial numbered pills within serial number consumer boxes, in serial numbered cases on serial numbered skids throughout the entire supply chain.

Is such forced supply chain integration good for small and mid-sized manufacturers? That remains to be seen and depends on who controls the access to the information and their motives. Even large brand owners have had their manufacturing locations, processes and costs examined by their large retail customers. Those retailers may request you make changes in your suppliers or recipes with an eye toward pursuing "lower prices" every year. The influence of customers is already a factor you may deal with. This is just another step toward transparency.

While the goal may be to increase food safety for the consumer, depending on the control and access to this important information that is afforded to government or influential retailers, the results could be used to gain political or economic advantages instead of the original goal of benefiting consumers.

The more a retailer knows about your processes and your ingredient sources, the more they are able to have it duplicated should they decide that they don't want to deal with you anymore. But realistically, between the internet and a lab, it is often easy to reverse engineer a product and then source suppliers of ingredients worldwide. Further, with such knowledge retailers could more easily make ingredient substitution 'requests' or even 'suggest' alternative suppliers to 'help' bring the cost of manufacturing your product down.

There are potential privacy issues that would need to be addressed for manufacturers to feel comfortable sharing information with their customers. If a blockchain were to reside on US servers and food manufacturers worldwide were to either provide access to their traceability information or contribute information to the blockchain, what's to say that in the event of a recall, that a foreign government wouldn't choose to seize the data, in their public's interest, to conduct a recall, or audit companies along that chain, or put restrictions on the buying from your company or country? It's not that they would necessarily choose to do this, but information is power and we need to be aware of where the power resides.

Cloud solutions, whether they are for consolidated traceability purposes or as a hosting method for software used for tracking, will generally hold data in a particular data centre or group of data centres, in a particular country. One of the most important questions I would have for any cloud provider or if you choose to host your system in a data centre is, "In what country is my data going to be stored?"

Data centres within on country will sometimes switch over to servers in other countries during maintenance or send copies of your data to other centres, such as partner centres in the other countries, as backups, in case there are problems at the local data centre. While this is a valid risk management strategy on their part, so you don't lose any of your data due to a hardware or power failure in one centre, if data is being moved around from country to country, be aware that countries, such as the US and Canada, have different privacy laws. So, for privacy risk management, if you are considering a cloud hosted solution for managing your food company, I suggest you do the research on the potential suppliers and decide if you are comfortable with the privacy policy of the country where your data may be stored.

Since you likely can't significantly affect the direction this information sharing process is taking, I suggest you begin to think about how sharing information with your customers or suppliers could benefit you. Social trends such as sustainability, calculating your carbon footprint and confirming product is sourced locally all require traceability. While those are emerging movements or consumer requests, to prove (or certify) any claims, you require a foundation of solid traceability. There are many reasons to jump on the traceability bandwagon now.

Technology and transparency will shape the way you manufacture in the future. The companies who succeed in this new reality will be those who find a way to embrace the inevitable openness of their manufacturing practices to the world. If you accept the power and role the consumer can and will play with social media, and aim to use the vast information available to you to adapt and tailor your product offering to the ever-changing needs of the marketplace, you will be well primed for success.

Customers want to know what they are eating and how it was made. So, use this to your advantage, get control of your plant and warehouse and then tell your story to customers about what you do to produce the best and safest product for them.

# Chapter 15. Ten Steps to get your traceability information working for you

In this book, I have shared stories about companies who have found ways to collect and use traceability for increased success. I've also gone through why you would want to connect traceability information, beyond just satisfying your inspector. Now is the time for action.

To tackle traceability in your manufacturing facility and warehouse, and ensure the information you are gathering is working for you, I've created this 10 Step Action Plan and the tools you'll need to assess and improve the traceability systems at your facility.

## Your 10 Step Action Plan

1) **Assess** your business using the Traceability Factor Excel tool available by emailing me at judith@traceabilitymatters.com Determine your starting score out of 100, including how many systems and silos currently exist with your data (what information is connected or disconnected), what your warehouse barcode readiness is and what benefits beyond traceability you are achieving now.

2) **Test** your recall abilities and the time it takes you to do a recall today. I suggest you try this with one of your most complicated products, one with multiple ingredients, several steps and one where production takes multiple days to complete (if applicable). Do this both from the raw material direction and from the finished good direction. Can you get the full information within minutes?

3) **Talk** to your staff and customers about what information they wish they had from you and aren't getting now (if any) and what formats they would ideally want to receive that

information in (electronic files through EDI, 1D or 2D barcode labels, RFID tags, etc.)

4) **Ask** your suppliers if they can help make receiving more efficient for you (including providing labels with GS1-128 barcodes including the relevant segments in a useful format, sending Certificate of Analysis, EDI documents, etc.)

5) **Investigate** technology options and brainstorm ideas for how you can remove the silos, reduce the number of systems you use and connect all the data pieces. I encourage you to contact me for suggestions

6) **Educate** your staff on traceability (do this regularly depending on your staff turnover) so that production floor and warehouse workers know how important their attention to detail is to the success of your business and recall plan. (if you want help with educating staff on traceability, talk to me or visit my website www.traceabilitymatters.com)

7) **Implement** processes and technologies to reduce the number of systems in place, get your traceability information into an electronic format and ensure your customers have the information they need in the format they prefer

8) **Re-test** your recall abilities and the time it takes to do a recall

9) **Re-assess** your Traceability Factor using the assessment tool

10) **Repeat** the above process on a regular basis (once a year at minimum) as there are always ways to improve and streamline processes and new customer requests to meet.

Time is money and as a business owner I understand that. If you are too busy running your company or would prefer to have an independent expert conduct the assessment for you and recommend tools and methods for your business to improve its traceability factor, my company **Traceability Matters** is happy to offer you this service.

Visit my website at www.traceabilitymatters.com for details.

Let me put to work my years of experience to assess your starting position and propose practical improvements and an action plan for how you can go from where you are now, to successfully tackling traceability and getting that information working for you for better profits.

I'll come onsite, observe your production process, walk through your warehouse, ask the right questions and provide a report with your score and suggested ideas that seem doable in your unique work environment. While best practices are great, the reality is that each business is unique, has different space restrictions and people resources available and any solution needs to adapt to your situation.

I understand that!

## Your biggest challenge – change management

I'd like to share one final story. It is the story of Uncle Joe. My experience working with manufacturers has primarily been with privately owned companies, the majority of which are family businesses. I've worked over 25 years in a family business, which is now multi-generational, so I understand family business dynamics. In nearly every family business, there is an Uncle Joe. He's been with the company forever (or so it seems, often it is more than 20 years) and is often a member of the family who owns the business.

143

Uncle Joe may not love computers and doesn't necessarily want to change how he does things. Nearly every family business I've worked with has their own Uncle Joe. So how do you manage Uncle Joe when things need to change to keep up with the new realities of business?

Recognize that Uncle Joe is often a key influencer, even if he doesn't manage a large staff; he may quietly provide leadership, by example, to many long-time staff. It is critical for successful change management that you get Uncle Joe on board with the changes you need to make to get your new system working for you. If your staff see Uncle Joe trying to make a change and getting on board with new requirements, they will often follow suit.

The best way we have found to manage Uncle Joe is to be open to customizing your information capture tool around the way he thinks. Recognize that different generations interact with technology differently. Perhaps he holds lots of information in his head or collects many of the needed pieces on paper or on a white board. Be open to how he does things and work with your technology provider to create a screen that looks like his paper or white board to allow him to enter information in a way that makes sense to him. Or, if he can't successfully enter it himself because he won't try or doesn't have the typing skills (hunt and peck typists can find computers an exercise in frustration) arrange for someone else to enter the information and produce a printout that looks like his own worksheet for Uncle Joe to check. Either way, it shows that you recognize his value and the way he does things.

One thing I have learned from watching my three sons interact with technology, is that each generation thinks differently when it comes to technology, whether it be a cell phone, a scanner or a computer. If we try to understand and accept that different generations will interact successfully with technology in different ways, we stand a better chance of truly making change happen in multi-generational environments.

That's one reason why I encourage you to invest in traceability training for everyone from your purchaser to your plant and warehouse staff, not just those in your food safety department. I also suggest you include key warehouse and production staff in your discussions about what information you need to collect, why it is needed and solicit their ideas for practical ways to gather that information. If they feel part of the process, they will feel more responsible to make it work when the solution is introduced. All of us like to understand why we are doing something and to know that what we are doing has larger significance. It gives our jobs and lives more meaning.

There is no one right way to tackle traceability challenges. Any solution must be doable for the people you have on board or you must be willing to add the right new people to get what you want. Staff members have the ability to sabotage any of your new ideas, even if they do so passively. Garbage In, Garbage Out will always hold true. To ensure that the information going into your system is accurate, reward the behaviour that you want to keep seeing. Challenge your staff to catch supplier mistakes and reward them for doing so. Every mistake caught is one less that you bring forward into your own system. Invest in training your staff on new technology so that they can help you get the information you need to grow your business.

If you've had success using some of these ideas to change processes for the better in your company, I hope that you will share those with others. Tell your customers about your increased traceability and use that story as a selling feature for why they should buy your products over your competition.

I also hope that you will share your success story with other businesses. Together, we can create stronger businesses that can compete successfully in our global marketplace.

## Track. Connect. Succeed.

### The Traceability Factor Assessment

Step 1 of my Action plan recommends you assess your business using my Traceability Factor Assessment Tool, an Excel spreadsheet that can help you evaluate your internal systems.

**The traceability flow** consists of the following critical points and that is what the Traceability Factor Assessment aims to evaluate and help you improve.

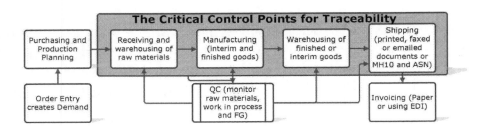

By answering the questions in the spreadsheet, you will receive a score out of 100 for how well your traceability information is working for you. This tool doesn't rate if you have traceability, I assume as a food company you have it, even if it is in paper logs. Instead, it looks at whether the information you are collecting is working to give you business advantages, both for recall and beyond. On the second tab of the Excel sheet you will find ways to quantify how one system or at least connecting pieces of technology can financially benefit your business. Use the ideas provided to create an expected ROI for your project. By doing so you will establish specific non-recall target goals you can work toward to become more profitable.

To ensure this assessment tool is relevant and up to date, I have chosen to make it available by email. That way, I can continually adapt it as I learn what information is useful in helping you get from where you are now to where you want to go. To request a copy, email me at judith@traceabilitymatters.com

**My final advice**: reduce the silos of information in your business and you will connect the dots for success. Use information as your competitive advantage. Understand your costs, your yields, what makes them vary and what products and customers are the most profitable for you overall. **Traceability can be used as a key differentiator for your future success**.

## How to use the GS1 Application Identifier List

The following list will help you decode barcodes in your warehouse so that you know what information your suppliers are providing to you in their barcodes. This can help you decide if a particular item would need to be relabelled or if the existing barcode would be sufficient for scanning to provide you with the information you need.

For traceability purposes, there are three segments which you should particularly look for. They are segment (10) lot number, segment (21) serial number and segment (11) production date (or another of the date segments). Those are the primary three segments that your suppliers will use if they issue you a recall. They will recall a lot number, one or more serial numbers or will ask for product to be returned that was produced or packaged on a particular date. If your GS1-128 barcode from your supplier does not contain one of those key fields, you'll likely have to relabel that product for traceability tracking in your facility.

Thank you to GS1 for giving me permission to include this list.

## Understanding the key fields on the GS1 list

The Application Identifier list consists of four columns. The first column contains the AI number, the second contains a description of the contents, the third contains information on how the contents should be formatted and the fourth is the Data Title, a shortened version of the description. Below I describe how to understand the first and third columns, as the descriptions and titles are self-explanatory.

## The Application Identifier (AI) Number

In reading this column, you'll need to understand how to read weights or any application identifiers you see on the list with (***) as part of the AI number.

Let's look at the Net Weight field, which is the 310*** AI from the list as an example.

| AI | Data Content | Format | Data Title |
|---|---|---|---|
| 310 (***) | Net weight, kilograms (Variable Measure Trade Item) | N4+N6 | NET WEIGHT (kg) |

The following GS1-128 includes a weight in the barcode.

(01)95012345678903(3103)000123

To decode this, you need to understand why the AI section reads (3103) instead of just (310) as shown in the AI list. It has to do with how decimals are handled in these barcodes. The N4 + N6 format for the 310(***) segment means that the AI header will actually be 4 digits long and the actual weight will be 6 digits long. The fourth digit of the 3103 barcode indicates the number of decimals included in the number (counting back from the far right of the number). So, for the barcode above 3103 means there are three decimals, so counting back three decimals in 000123 means the net weight for this item is 0.123kg.

Finally, if you find barcodes with AI numbers that are not listed on this list, they may be very new AI's or your supplier may be using those segments for internal information relevant to them. Most warehouse management systems can ignore AI sections that they don't recognize.

## The Format Column

Some of the AI sections are fixed width, meaning they will always contain a number of the exact length indicated in the **Format** column. The **Format** column tells you what the string on an actual label consists of.

It will always include the AI number (which is two numbers to four numbers long) plus the length of the actual information the company is sharing for that section. If the actual information says **N**6 it means it will be six **N**umbers. If the actual information says X..20 as it does for the (21) serial number AI, it means that the actual information could be a mix of numbers or letters and can be up to 20 characters in length. For example, the production date of January 16, 2014 will appear as follows on a GS1-128 barcode

11 140116 or (11) 140116

The **Format** of application identifier 11 is AI YYMMDD (or N2 + N6), where the AI (application identifier) is a two-digit Number that may be inside brackets or just separated from the actual information with a space and the date in six numbers following.

## The GS1 Application Identifier List

While the following list was current as of writing this book, as new needs for information are recognized around the world, GS1 may add additional segments. If you find segments in a barcode not on this list, visit the GS1 Website at www.gs1.org to check and see if that segment is a new field in a more recent version of the list. If not, ask your supplier what that segment is being used for; likely, it is being used as internal information for your supplier company.

| AI | Description | Format | Data Title |
|---|---|---|---|
| 00 | Serial Shipping Container Code (SSCC) | N2+N18 | SSCC |
| 01 | Global Trade Item Number (GTIN) | N2+N14 | GTIN |
| 02 | GTIN of contained trade items | N2+N14 | CONTENT |
| 10 | Batch or lot number | N2+X..20 | BATCH/LOT |
| 11 | Production date (YYMMDD) | N2+N6 | PROD DATE |
| 12 | Due date (YYMMDD) | N2+N6 | DUE DATE |
| 13 | Packaging date (YYMMDD) | N2+N6 | PACK DATE |
| 15 | Best before date (YYMMDD) | N2+N6 | BEST BEFORE or BEST BY |
| 16 | Sell by date (YYMMDD) | N2+N6 | SELL BY |
| 17 | Expiration date (YYMMDD) | N2+N6 | USE BY OR EXPIRY |
| 20 | Internal product variant | N2+N2 | VARIANT |
| 21 | Serial number | N2+X..20 | SERIAL |
| 22 | Consumer product variant | N2+X..20 | CPV |
| 235 | Third Party Controlled, Serialised Extension of GTIN (TPX) | N3+X..28 | TPX |
| 240 | Additional product identification assigned by the manufacturer | N3+X..30 | ADDITIONAL ID |
| 241 | Customer part number | N3+X..30 | CUST. PART NO. |
| 242 | Made-to-Order variation number | N3+N..6 | MTO VARIANT |
| 243 | Packaging component number | N3+X..20 | PCN |
| 250 | Secondary serial number | N3+X..30 | SECONDARY SERIAL |
| 251 | Reference to source entity | N3+X..30 | REF. TO SOURCE |
| 253 | Global Document Type Identifier (GDTI) | N3+N13+X..17 | GDTI |
| 254 | GLN extension component | N3+X..20 | GLN EXTENSION COMPONENT |
| 255 | Global Coupon Number (GCN) | N3+N13+N..12 | GCN |

| 30 | Variable count of items (variable measure trade item) | N2+N..8 | VAR. COUNT |
|---|---|---|---|
| 3100 | Net weight, kilograms (variable measure trade item) | N4+N6 | NET WEIGHT (kg) |
| 3101 | Net weight, kilograms (variable measure trade item) | N4+N6 | NET WEIGHT (kg) |
| 3102 | Net weight, kilograms (variable measure trade item) | N4+N6 | NET WEIGHT (kg) |
| 3103 | Net weight, kilograms (variable measure trade item) | N4+N6 | NET WEIGHT (kg) |
| 3104 | Net weight, kilograms (variable measure trade item) | N4+N6 | NET WEIGHT (kg) |
| 3105 | Net weight, kilograms (variable measure trade item) | N4+N6 | NET WEIGHT (kg) |
| 3110 | Length or first dimension, metres (variable measure trade item) | N4+N6 | LENGTH (m) |
| 3111 | Length or first dimension, metres (variable measure trade item) | N4+N6 | LENGTH (m) |
| 3112 | Length or first dimension, metres (variable measure trade item) | N4+N6 | LENGTH (m) |
| 3113 | Length or first dimension, metres (variable measure trade item) | N4+N6 | LENGTH (m) |
| 3114 | Length or first dimension, metres (variable measure trade item) | N4+N6 | LENGTH (m) |
| 3115 | Length or first dimension, metres (variable measure trade item) | N4+N6 | LENGTH (m) |
| 3120 | Width, diameter, or second dimension, metres (variable measure trade item) | N4+N6 | WIDTH (m) |
| 3121 | Width, diameter, or second dimension, metres (variable measure trade item) | N4+N6 | WIDTH (m) |
| 3122 | Width, diameter, or second dimension, metres (variable measure trade item) | N4+N6 | WIDTH (m) |
| 3123 | Width, diameter, or second dimension, metres (variable | N4+N6 | WIDTH (m) |

| | measure trade item) | | |
|---|---|---|---|
| **3124** | **Width, diameter, or second dimension, metres (variable measure trade item)** | **N4+N6** | **WIDTH (m)** |
| 3125 | Width, diameter, or second dimension, metres (variable measure trade item) | N4+N6 | WIDTH (m) |
| **3130** | **Depth, thickness, height, or third dimension, metres (variable measure trade item)** | **N4+N6** | **HEIGHT (m)** |
| 3131 | Depth, thickness, height, or third dimension, metres (variable measure trade item) | N4+N6 | HEIGHT (m) |
| **3132** | **Depth, thickness, height, or third dimension, metres (variable measure trade item)** | **N4+N6** | **HEIGHT (m)** |
| 3133 | Depth, thickness, height, or third dimension, metres (variable measure trade item) | N4+N6 | HEIGHT (m) |
| **3134** | **Depth, thickness, height, or third dimension, metres (variable measure trade item)** | **N4+N6** | **HEIGHT (m)** |
| 3135 | Depth, thickness, height, or third dimension, metres (variable measure trade item) | N4+N6 | HEIGHT (m) |
| **3140** | **Area, square metres (variable measure trade item)** | **N4+N6** | **AREA (m2)** |
| 3141 | Area, square metres (variable measure trade item) | N4+N6 | AREA (m2) |
| **3142** | **Area, square metres (variable measure trade item)** | **N4+N6** | **AREA (m2)** |
| 3143 | Area, square metres (variable measure trade item) | N4+N6 | AREA (m2) |
| **3144** | **Area, square metres (variable measure trade item)** | **N4+N6** | **AREA (m2)** |
| 3145 | Area, square metres (variable measure trade item) | N4+N6 | AREA (m2) |
| **3150** | **Net volume, litres (variable measure trade item)** | **N4+N6** | **NET VOLUME (l)** |
| 3151 | Net volume, litres (variable measure trade item) | N4+N6 | NET VOLUME (l) |

| 3152 | Net volume, litres (variable measure trade item) | N4+N6 | NET VOLUME (l) |
|------|--------------------------------------------------|-------|----------------|
| 3153 | Net volume, litres (variable measure trade item) | N4+N6 | NET VOLUME (l) |
| 3154 | Net volume, litres (variable measure trade item) | N4+N6 | NET VOLUME (l) |
| 3155 | Net volume, litres (variable measure trade item) | N4+N6 | NET VOLUME (l) |
| 3160 | Net volume, cubic metres (variable measure trade item) | N4+N6 | NET VOLUME (m3) |
| 3161 | Net volume, cubic metres (variable measure trade item) | N4+N6 | NET VOLUME (m3) |
| 3162 | Net volume, cubic metres (variable measure trade item) | N4+N6 | NET VOLUME (m3) |
| 3163 | Net volume, cubic metres (variable measure trade item) | N4+N6 | NET VOLUME (m3) |
| 3164 | Net volume, cubic metres (variable measure trade item) | N4+N6 | NET VOLUME (m3) |
| 3165 | Net volume, cubic metres (variable measure trade item) | N4+N6 | NET VOLUME (m3) |
| 3200 | Net weight, pounds (variable measure trade item) | N4+N6 | NET WEIGHT (lb) |
| 3201 | Net weight, pounds (variable measure trade item) | N4+N6 | NET WEIGHT (lb) |
| 3202 | Net weight, pounds (variable measure trade item) | N4+N6 | NET WEIGHT (lb) |
| 3203 | Net weight, pounds (variable measure trade item) | N4+N6 | NET WEIGHT (lb) |
| 3204 | Net weight, pounds (variable measure trade item) | N4+N6 | NET WEIGHT (lb) |
| 3205 | Net weight, pounds (variable measure trade item) | N4+N6 | NET WEIGHT (lb) |
| 3210 | Length or first dimension, inches (variable measure trade item) | N4+N6 | LENGTH (in) |
| 3211 | Length or first dimension, inches (variable measure trade item) | N4+N6 | LENGTH (in) |
| 3212 | Length or first dimension, inches (variable measure trade item) | N4+N6 | LENGTH (in) |
| 3213 | Length or first dimension, inches (variable measure trade item) | N4+N6 | LENGTH (in) |
| 3214 | Length or first dimension, inches (variable measure trade item) | N4+N6 | LENGTH (in) |

| 3215 | Length or first dimension, inches (variable measure trade item) | N4+N6 | LENGTH (in) |
|------|------|------|------|
| 3220 | Length or first dimension, feet (variable measure trade item) | N4+N6 | LENGTH (ft) |
| 3221 | Length or first dimension, feet (variable measure trade item) | N4+N6 | LENGTH (ft) |
| 3222 | Length or first dimension, feet (variable measure trade item) | N4+N6 | LENGTH (ft) |
| 3223 | Length or first dimension, feet (variable measure trade item) | N4+N6 | LENGTH (ft) |
| 3224 | Length or first dimension, feet (variable measure trade item) | N4+N6 | LENGTH (ft) |
| 3225 | Length or first dimension, feet (variable measure trade item) | N4+N6 | LENGTH (ft) |
| 3230 | Length or first dimension, yards (variable measure trade item) | N4+N6 | LENGTH (yd) |
| 3231 | Length or first dimension, yards (variable measure trade item) | N4+N6 | LENGTH (yd) |
| 3232 | Length or first dimension, yards (variable measure trade item) | N4+N6 | LENGTH (yd) |
| 3233 | Length or first dimension, yards (variable measure trade item) | N4+N6 | LENGTH (yd) |
| 3234 | Length or first dimension, yards (variable measure trade item) | N4+N6 | LENGTH (yd) |
| 3235 | Length or first dimension, yards (variable measure trade item) | N4+N6 | LENGTH (yd) |
| 3240 | Width, diameter, or second dimension, inches (variable measure trade item) | N4+N6 | WIDTH (in) |
| 3241 | Width, diameter, or second dimension, inches (variable measure trade item) | N4+N6 | WIDTH (in) |
| 3242 | Width, diameter, or second dimension, inches (variable measure trade item) | N4+N6 | WIDTH (in) |
| 3243 | Width, diameter, or second dimension, inches (variable measure trade item) | N4+N6 | WIDTH (in) |
| 3244 | Width, diameter, or second dimension, inches (variable measure trade item) | N4+N6 | WIDTH (in) |
| 3245 | Width, diameter, or second dimension, inches (variable | N4+N6 | WIDTH (in) |

| | measure trade item) | | |
|------|---------------------------------------------------------------------|-------|-------------|
| 3250 | Width, diameter, or second dimension, feet (variable measure trade item) | N4+N6 | WIDTH (ft) |
| 3251 | Width, diameter, or second dimension, feet (variable measure trade item) | N4+N6 | WIDTH (ft) |
| 3252 | Width, diameter, or second dimension, feet (variable measure trade item) | N4+N6 | WIDTH (ft) |
| 3253 | Width, diameter, or second dimension, feet (variable measure trade item) | N4+N6 | WIDTH (ft) |
| 3254 | Width, diameter, or second dimension, feet (variable measure trade item) | N4+N6 | WIDTH (ft) |
| 3255 | Width, diameter, or second dimension, feet (variable measure trade item) | N4+N6 | WIDTH (ft) |
| 3260 | Width, diameter, or second dimension, yards (variable measure trade item) | N4+N6 | WIDTH (yd) |
| 3261 | Width, diameter, or second dimension, yards (variable measure trade item) | N4+N6 | WIDTH (yd) |
| 3262 | Width, diameter, or second dimension, yards (variable measure trade item) | N4+N6 | WIDTH (yd) |
| 3263 | Width, diameter, or second dimension, yards (variable measure trade item) | N4+N6 | WIDTH (yd) |
| 3264 | Width, diameter, or second dimension, yards (variable measure trade item) | N4+N6 | WIDTH (yd) |
| 3265 | Width, diameter, or second dimension, yards (variable measure trade item) | N4+N6 | WIDTH (yd) |
| 3270 | Depth, thickness, height, or third dimension, inches (variable measure trade item) | N4+N6 | HEIGHT (in) |
| 3271 | Depth, thickness, height, or third dimension, inches (variable | N4+N6 | HEIGHT (in) |

| | | | |
|---|---|---|---|
| | measure trade item) | | |
| 3272 | Depth, thickness, height, or third dimension, inches (variable measure trade item) | N4+N6 | HEIGHT (in) |
| 3273 | Depth, thickness, height, or third dimension, inches (variable measure trade item) | N4+N6 | HEIGHT (in) |
| 3274 | Depth, thickness, height, or third dimension, inches (variable measure trade item) | N4+N6 | HEIGHT (in) |
| 3275 | Depth, thickness, height, or third dimension, inches (variable measure trade item) | N4+N6 | HEIGHT (in) |
| 3280 | Depth, thickness, height, or third dimension, feet (variable measure trade item) | N4+N6 | HEIGHT (ft) |
| 3281 | Depth, thickness, height, or third dimension, feet (variable measure trade item) | N4+N6 | HEIGHT (ft) |
| 3282 | Depth, thickness, height, or third dimension, feet (variable measure trade item) | N4+N6 | HEIGHT (ft) |
| 3283 | Depth, thickness, height, or third dimension, feet (variable measure trade item) | N4+N6 | HEIGHT (ft) |
| 3284 | Depth, thickness, height, or third dimension, feet (variable measure trade item) | N4+N6 | HEIGHT (ft) |
| 3285 | Depth, thickness, height, or third dimension, feet (variable measure trade item) | N4+N6 | HEIGHT (ft) |
| 3290 | Depth, thickness, height, or third dimension, yards (variable measure trade item) | N4+N6 | HEIGHT (yd) |
| 3291 | Depth, thickness, height, or third dimension, yards (variable measure trade item) | N4+N6 | HEIGHT (yd) |
| 3292 | Depth, thickness, height, or third dimension, yards (variable measure trade item) | N4+N6 | HEIGHT (yd) |
| 3293 | Depth, thickness, height, or third dimension, yards (variable | N4+N6 | HEIGHT (yd) |

| | measure trade item) | | |
|------|------|------|------|
| 3294 | Depth, thickness, height, or third dimension, yards (variable measure trade item) | N4+N6 | HEIGHT (yd) |
| 3295 | Depth, thickness, height, or third dimension, yards (variable measure trade item) | N4+N6 | HEIGHT (yd) |
| 3300 | Logistic weight, kilograms | N4+N6 | GROSS WEIGHT (kg) |
| 3301 | Logistic weight, kilograms | N4+N6 | GROSS WEIGHT (kg) |
| 3302 | Logistic weight, kilograms | N4+N6 | GROSS WEIGHT (kg) |
| 3303 | Logistic weight, kilograms | N4+N6 | GROSS WEIGHT (kg) |
| 3304 | Logistic weight, kilograms | N4+N6 | GROSS WEIGHT (kg) |
| 3305 | Logistic weight, kilograms | N4+N6 | GROSS WEIGHT (kg) |
| 3310 | Length or first dimension, metres | N4+N6 | LENGTH (m), log |
| 3311 | Length or first dimension, metres | N4+N6 | LENGTH (m), log |
| 3312 | Length or first dimension, metres | N4+N6 | LENGTH (m), log |
| 3313 | Length or first dimension, metres | N4+N6 | LENGTH (m), log |
| 3314 | Length or first dimension, metres | N4+N6 | LENGTH (m), log |
| 3315 | Length or first dimension, metres | N4+N6 | LENGTH (m), log |
| 3320 | Width, diameter, or second dimension, metres | N4+N6 | WIDTH (m), log |
| 3321 | Width, diameter, or second dimension, metres | N4+N6 | WIDTH (m), log |
| 3322 | Width, diameter, or second dimension, metres | N4+N6 | WIDTH (m), log |
| 3323 | Width, diameter, or second dimension, metres | N4+N6 | WIDTH (m), log |
| 3324 | Width, diameter, or second dimension, metres | N4+N6 | WIDTH (m), log |
| 3325 | Width, diameter, or second dimension, metres | N4+N6 | WIDTH (m), log |
| 3330 | Depth, thickness, height, or third | N4+N6 | HEIGHT (m), log |

| | | | |
|---|---|---|---|
| | dimension, metres | | |
| 3331 | Depth, thickness, height, or third dimension, metres | N4+N6 | HEIGHT (m), log |
| 3332 | Depth, thickness, height, or third dimension, metres | N4+N6 | HEIGHT (m), log |
| 3333 | Depth, thickness, height, or third dimension, metres | N4+N6 | HEIGHT (m), log |
| 3334 | Depth, thickness, height, or third dimension, metres | N4+N6 | HEIGHT (m), log |
| 3335 | Depth, thickness, height, or third dimension, metres | N4+N6 | HEIGHT (m), log |
| 3340 | Area, square metres | N4+N6 | AREA (m2), log |
| 3341 | Area, square metres | N4+N6 | AREA (m2), log |
| 3342 | Area, square metres | N4+N6 | AREA (m2), log |
| 3343 | Area, square metres | N4+N6 | AREA (m2), log |
| 3344 | Area, square metres | N4+N6 | AREA (m2), log |
| 3345 | Area, square metres | N4+N6 | AREA (m2), log |
| 3350 | Logistic volume, litres | N4+N6 | VOLUME (l), log |
| 3351 | Logistic volume, litres | N4+N6 | VOLUME (l), log |
| 3352 | Logistic volume, litres | N4+N6 | VOLUME (l), log |
| 3353 | Logistic volume, litres | N4+N6 | VOLUME (l), log |
| 3354 | Logistic volume, litres | N4+N6 | VOLUME (l), log |
| 3355 | Logistic volume, litres | N4+N6 | VOLUME (l), log |
| 3360 | Logistic volume, cubic metres | N4+N6 | VOLUME (m3), log |
| 3361 | Logistic volume, cubic metres | N4+N6 | VOLUME (m3), log |
| 3362 | Logistic volume, cubic metres | N4+N6 | VOLUME (m3), log |
| 3363 | Logistic volume, cubic metres | N4+N6 | VOLUME (m3), log |
| 3364 | Logistic volume, cubic metres | N4+N6 | VOLUME (m3), log |
| 3365 | Logistic volume, cubic metres | N4+N6 | VOLUME (m3), log |
| 3370 | Kilograms per square metre | N4+N6 | KG PER m2 |

| | | | |
|---|---|---|---|
| 3371 | Kilograms per square metre | N4+N6 | KG PER m2 |
| 3372 | Kilograms per square metre | N4+N6 | KG PER m2 |
| 3373 | Kilograms per square metre | N4+N6 | KG PER m2 |
| 3374 | Kilograms per square metre | N4+N6 | KG PER m2 |
| 3375 | Kilograms per square metre | N4+N6 | KG PER m2 |
| 3400 | Logistic weight, pounds | N4+N6 | GROSS WEIGHT (lb) |
| 3401 | Logistic weight, pounds | N4+N6 | GROSS WEIGHT (lb) |
| 3402 | Logistic weight, pounds | N4+N6 | GROSS WEIGHT (lb) |
| 3403 | Logistic weight, pounds | N4+N6 | GROSS WEIGHT (lb) |
| 3404 | Logistic weight, pounds | N4+N6 | GROSS WEIGHT (lb) |
| 3405 | Logistic weight, pounds | N4+N6 | GROSS WEIGHT (lb) |
| 3410 | Length or first dimension, inches | N4+N6 | LENGTH (in), log |
| 3411 | Length or first dimension, inches | N4+N6 | LENGTH (in), log |
| 3412 | Length or first dimension, inches | N4+N6 | LENGTH (in), log |
| 3413 | Length or first dimension, inches | N4+N6 | LENGTH (in), log |
| 3414 | Length or first dimension, inches | N4+N6 | LENGTH (in), log |
| 3415 | Length or first dimension, inches | N4+N6 | LENGTH (in), log |
| 3420 | Length or first dimension, feet | N4+N6 | LENGTH (ft), log |
| 3421 | Length or first dimension, feet | N4+N6 | LENGTH (ft), log |
| 3422 | Length or first dimension, feet | N4+N6 | LENGTH (ft), log |
| 3423 | Length or first dimension, feet | N4+N6 | LENGTH (ft), log |
| 3424 | Length or first dimension, feet | N4+N6 | LENGTH (ft), log |
| 3425 | Length or first dimension, feet | N4+N6 | LENGTH (ft), log |
| 3430 | Length or first dimension, yards | N4+N6 | LENGTH (yd), log |
| 3431 | Length or first dimension, yards | N4+N6 | LENGTH (yd), log |
| 3432 | Length or first dimension, yards | N4+N6 | LENGTH (yd), log |

| 3433 | Length or first dimension, yards | N4+N6 | LENGTH (yd), log |
|------|----------------------------------|-------|------------------|
| 3434 | Length or first dimension, yards | N4+N6 | LENGTH (yd), log |
| 3435 | Length or first dimension, yards | N4+N6 | LENGTH (yd), log |
| 3440 | Width, diameter, or second dimension, inches | N4+N6 | WIDTH (in), log |
| 3441 | Width, diameter, or second dimension, inches | N4+N6 | WIDTH (in), log |
| 3442 | Width, diameter, or second dimension, inches | N4+N6 | WIDTH (in), log |
| 3443 | Width, diameter, or second dimension, inches | N4+N6 | WIDTH (in), log |
| 3444 | Width, diameter, or second dimension, inches | N4+N6 | WIDTH (in), log |
| 3445 | Width, diameter, or second dimension, inches | N4+N6 | WIDTH (in), log |
| 3450 | Width, diameter, or second dimension, feet | N4+N6 | WIDTH (ft), log |
| 3451 | Width, diameter, or second dimension, feet | N4+N6 | WIDTH (ft), log |
| 3452 | Width, diameter, or second dimension, feet | N4+N6 | WIDTH (ft), log |
| 3453 | Width, diameter, or second dimension, feet | N4+N6 | WIDTH (ft), log |
| 3454 | Width, diameter, or second dimension, feet | N4+N6 | WIDTH (ft), log |
| 3455 | Width, diameter, or second dimension, feet | N4+N6 | WIDTH (ft), log |
| 3460 | Width, diameter, or second dimension, yard | N4+N6 | WIDTH (yd), log |
| 3461 | Width, diameter, or second dimension, yard | N4+N6 | WIDTH (yd), log |
| 3462 | Width, diameter, or second dimension, yard | N4+N6 | WIDTH (yd), log |
| 3463 | Width, diameter, or second dimension, yard | N4+N6 | WIDTH (yd), log |
| 3464 | Width, diameter, or second dimension, yard | N4+N6 | WIDTH (yd), log |
| 3465 | Width, diameter, or second dimension, yard | N4+N6 | WIDTH (yd), log |
| 3470 | Depth, thickness, height, or third dimension, inches | N4+N6 | HEIGHT (in), log |

| 3471 | Depth, thickness, height, or third dimension, inches | N4+N6 | HEIGHT (in), log |
|---|---|---|---|
| 3472 | Depth, thickness, height, or third dimension, inches | N4+N6 | HEIGHT (in), log |
| 3473 | Depth, thickness, height, or third dimension, inches | N4+N6 | HEIGHT (in), log |
| 3474 | Depth, thickness, height, or third dimension, inches | N4+N6 | HEIGHT (in), log |
| 3475 | Depth, thickness, height, or third dimension, inches | N4+N6 | HEIGHT (in), log |
| 3480 | Depth, thickness, height, or third dimension, feet | N4+N6 | HEIGHT (ft), log |
| 3481 | Depth, thickness, height, or third dimension, feet | N4+N6 | HEIGHT (ft), log |
| 3482 | Depth, thickness, height, or third dimension, feet | N4+N6 | HEIGHT (ft), log |
| 3483 | Depth, thickness, height, or third dimension, feet | N4+N6 | HEIGHT (ft), log |
| 3484 | Depth, thickness, height, or third dimension, feet | N4+N6 | HEIGHT (ft), log |
| 3485 | Depth, thickness, height, or third dimension, feet | N4+N6 | HEIGHT (ft), log |
| 3490 | Depth, thickness, height, or third dimension, yards | N4+N6 | HEIGHT (yd), log |
| 3491 | Depth, thickness, height, or third dimension, yards | N4+N6 | HEIGHT (yd), log |
| 3492 | Depth, thickness, height, or third dimension, yards | N4+N6 | HEIGHT (yd), log |
| 3493 | Depth, thickness, height, or third dimension, yards | N4+N6 | HEIGHT (yd), log |
| 3494 | Depth, thickness, height, or third dimension, yards | N4+N6 | HEIGHT (yd), log |
| 3495 | Depth, thickness, height, or third dimension, yards | N4+N6 | HEIGHT (yd), log |
| 3500 | Area, square inches (variable measure trade item) | N4+N6 | AREA (in2) |
| 3501 | Area, square inches (variable measure trade item) | N4+N6 | AREA (in2) |
| 3502 | Area, square inches (variable measure trade item) | N4+N6 | AREA (in2) |
| 3503 | Area, square inches (variable measure trade item) | N4+N6 | AREA (in2) |

| 3504 | Area, square inches (variable measure trade item) | N4+N6 | AREA (in2) |
|---|---|---|---|
| 3505 | Area, square inches (variable measure trade item) | N4+N6 | AREA (in2) |
| 3510 | Area, square feet (variable measure trade item) | N4+N6 | AREA (ft2) |
| 3511 | Area, square feet (variable measure trade item) | N4+N6 | AREA (ft2) |
| 3512 | Area, square feet (variable measure trade item) | N4+N6 | AREA (ft2) |
| 3513 | Area, square feet (variable measure trade item) | N4+N6 | AREA (ft2) |
| 3514 | Area, square feet (variable measure trade item) | N4+N6 | AREA (ft2) |
| 3515 | Area, square feet (variable measure trade item) | N4+N6 | AREA (ft2) |
| 3520 | Area, square yards (variable measure trade item) | N4+N6 | AREA (yd2) |
| 3521 | Area, square yards (variable measure trade item) | N4+N6 | AREA (yd2) |
| 3522 | Area, square yards (variable measure trade item) | N4+N6 | AREA (yd2) |
| 3523 | Area, square yards (variable measure trade item) | N4+N6 | AREA (yd2) |
| 3524 | Area, square yards (variable measure trade item) | N4+N6 | AREA (yd2) |
| 3525 | Area, square yards (variable measure trade item) | N4+N6 | AREA (yd2) |
| 3530 | Area, square inches | N4+N6 | AREA (in2), log |
| 3531 | Area, square inches | N4+N6 | AREA (in2), log |
| 3532 | Area, square inches | N4+N6 | AREA (in2), log |
| 3533 | Area, square inches | N4+N6 | AREA (in2), log |
| 3534 | Area, square inches | N4+N6 | AREA (in2), log |
| 3535 | Area, square inches | N4+N6 | AREA (in2), log |
| 3540 | Area, square feet | N4+N6 | AREA (ft2), log |
| 3541 | Area, square feet | N4+N6 | AREA (ft2), log |
| 3542 | Area, square feet | N4+N6 | AREA (ft2), log |

| 3543 | Area, square feet | N4+N6 | AREA (ft2), log |
|------|------------------|-------|-----------------|
| 3544 | Area, square feet | N4+N6 | AREA (ft2), log |
| 3545 | Area, square feet | N4+N6 | AREA (ft2), log |
| 3550 | Area, square yards | N4+N6 | AREA (yd2), log |
| 3551 | Area, square yards | N4+N6 | AREA (yd2), log |
| 3552 | Area, square yards | N4+N6 | AREA (yd2), log |
| 3553 | Area, square yards | N4+N6 | AREA (yd2), log |
| 3554 | Area, square yards | N4+N6 | AREA (yd2), log |
| 3555 | Area, square yards | N4+N6 | AREA (yd2), log |
| 3560 | Net weight, troy ounces (variable measure trade item) | N4+N6 | NET WEIGHT (t oz) |
| 3561 | Net weight, troy ounces (variable measure trade item) | N4+N6 | NET WEIGHT (t oz) |
| 3562 | Net weight, troy ounces (variable measure trade item) | N4+N6 | NET WEIGHT (t oz) |
| 3563 | Net weight, troy ounces (variable measure trade item) | N4+N6 | NET WEIGHT (t oz) |
| 3564 | Net weight, troy ounces (variable measure trade item) | N4+N6 | NET WEIGHT (t oz) |
| 3565 | Net weight, troy ounces (variable measure trade item) | N4+N6 | NET WEIGHT (t oz) |
| 3570 | Net weight (or volume), ounces (variable measure trade item) | N4+N6 | NET VOLUME (oz) |
| 3571 | Net weight (or volume), ounces (variable measure trade item) | N4+N6 | NET VOLUME (oz) |
| 3572 | Net weight (or volume), ounces (variable measure trade item) | N4+N6 | NET VOLUME (oz) |
| 3573 | Net weight (or volume), ounces (variable measure trade item) | N4+N6 | NET VOLUME (oz) |
| 3574 | Net weight (or volume), ounces (variable measure trade item) | N4+N6 | NET VOLUME (oz) |
| 3575 | Net weight (or volume), ounces (variable measure trade item) | N4+N6 | NET VOLUME (oz) |
| 3600 | Net volume, quarts (variable measure trade item) | N4+N6 | NET VOLUME (qt) |
| 3601 | Net volume, quarts (variable measure trade item) | N4+N6 | NET VOLUME (qt) |

| 3602 | Net volume, quarts (variable measure trade item) | N4+N6 | NET VOLUME (qt) |
|------|--------------------------------------------------|-------|-----------------|
| 3603 | Net volume, quarts (variable measure trade item) | N4+N6 | NET VOLUME (qt) |
| 3604 | Net volume, quarts (variable measure trade item) | N4+N6 | NET VOLUME (qt) |
| 3605 | Net volume, quarts (variable measure trade item) | N4+N6 | NET VOLUME (qt) |
| 3610 | Net volume, gallons U.S. (variable measure trade item) | N4+N6 | NET VOLUME (gal.) |
| 3611 | Net volume, gallons U.S. (variable measure trade item) | N4+N6 | NET VOLUME (gal.) |
| 3612 | Net volume, gallons U.S. (variable measure trade item) | N4+N6 | NET VOLUME (gal.) |
| 3613 | Net volume, gallons U.S. (variable measure trade item) | N4+N6 | NET VOLUME (gal.) |
| 3614 | Net volume, gallons U.S. (variable measure trade item) | N4+N6 | NET VOLUME (gal.) |
| 3615 | Net volume, gallons U.S. (variable measure trade item) | N4+N6 | NET VOLUME (gal.) |
| 3620 | Logistic volume, quarts | N4+N6 | VOLUME (qt), log |
| 3621 | Logistic volume, quarts | N4+N6 | VOLUME (qt), log |
| 3622 | Logistic volume, quarts | N4+N6 | VOLUME (qt), log |
| 3623 | Logistic volume, quarts | N4+N6 | VOLUME (qt), log |
| 3624 | Logistic volume, quarts | N4+N6 | VOLUME (qt), log |
| 3625 | Logistic volume, quarts | N4+N6 | VOLUME (qt), log |
| 3630 | Logistic volume, gallons U.S. | N4+N6 | VOLUME (gal.), log |
| 3631 | Logistic volume, gallons U.S. | N4+N6 | VOLUME (gal.), log |
| 3632 | Logistic volume, gallons U.S. | N4+N6 | VOLUME (gal.), log |
| 3633 | Logistic volume, gallons U.S. | N4+N6 | VOLUME (gal.), log |
| 3634 | Logistic volume, gallons U.S. | N4+N6 | VOLUME (gal.), log |
| 3635 | Logistic volume, gallons U.S. | N4+N6 | VOLUME (gal.), log |
| 3640 | Net volume, cubic inches (variable measure trade item) | N4+N6 | VOLUME (in3) |

| 3641 | Net volume, cubic inches (variable measure trade item) | N4+N6 | VOLUME (in3) |
|------|--------------------------------------------------------|-------|--------------|
| 3642 | Net volume, cubic inches (variable measure trade item) | N4+N6 | VOLUME (in3) |
| 3643 | Net volume, cubic inches (variable measure trade item) | N4+N6 | VOLUME (in3) |
| 3644 | Net volume, cubic inches (variable measure trade item) | N4+N6 | VOLUME (in3) |
| 3645 | Net volume, cubic inches (variable measure trade item) | N4+N6 | VOLUME (in3) |
| 3650 | Net volume, cubic feet (variable measure trade item) | N4+N6 | VOLUME (ft3) |
| 3651 | Net volume, cubic feet (variable measure trade item) | N4+N6 | VOLUME (ft3) |
| 3652 | Net volume, cubic feet (variable measure trade item) | N4+N6 | VOLUME (ft3) |
| 3653 | Net volume, cubic feet (variable measure trade item) | N4+N6 | VOLUME (ft3) |
| 3654 | Net volume, cubic feet (variable measure trade item) | N4+N6 | VOLUME (ft3) |
| 3655 | Net volume, cubic feet (variable measure trade item) | N4+N6 | VOLUME (ft3) |
| 3660 | Net volume, cubic yards (variable measure trade item) | N4+N6 | VOLUME (yd3) |
| 3661 | Net volume, cubic yards (variable measure trade item) | N4+N6 | VOLUME (yd3) |
| 3662 | Net volume, cubic yards (variable measure trade item) | N4+N6 | VOLUME (yd3) |
| 3663 | Net volume, cubic yards (variable measure trade item) | N4+N6 | VOLUME (yd3) |
| 3664 | Net volume, cubic yards (variable measure trade item) | N4+N6 | VOLUME (yd3) |
| 3665 | Net volume, cubic yards (variable measure trade item) | N4+N6 | VOLUME (yd3) |
| 3670 | Logistic volume, cubic inches | N4+N6 | VOLUME (in3), log |
| 3671 | Logistic volume, cubic inches | N4+N6 | VOLUME (in3), log |
| 3672 | Logistic volume, cubic inches | N4+N6 | VOLUME (in3), log |
| 3673 | Logistic volume, cubic inches | N4+N6 | VOLUME (in3), log |
| 3674 | Logistic volume, cubic inches | N4+N6 | VOLUME (in3), log |

| | | | |
|---|---|---|---|
| 3675 | Logistic volume, cubic inches | N4+N6 | VOLUME (in3), log |
| 3680 | Logistic volume, cubic feet | N4+N6 | VOLUME (ft3), log |
| 3681 | Logistic volume, cubic feet | N4+N6 | VOLUME (ft3), log |
| 3682 | Logistic volume, cubic feet | N4+N6 | VOLUME (ft3), log |
| 3683 | Logistic volume, cubic feet | N4+N6 | VOLUME (ft3), log |
| 3684 | Logistic volume, cubic feet | N4+N6 | VOLUME (ft3), log |
| 3685 | Logistic volume, cubic feet | N4+N6 | VOLUME (ft3), log |
| 3690 | Logistic volume, cubic yards | N4+N6 | VOLUME (yd3), log |
| 3691 | Logistic volume, cubic yards | N4+N6 | VOLUME (yd3), log |
| 3692 | Logistic volume, cubic yards | N4+N6 | VOLUME (yd3), log |
| 3693 | Logistic volume, cubic yards | N4+N6 | VOLUME (yd3), log |
| 3694 | Logistic volume, cubic yards | N4+N6 | VOLUME (yd3), log |
| 3695 | Logistic volume, cubic yards | N4+N6 | VOLUME (yd3), log |
| 37 | Count of trade items or trade item pieces contained in a logistic unit | N2+N..8 | COUNT |
| 3900 | Applicable amount payable or Coupon value, local currency | N4+N..15 | AMOUNT |
| 3901 | Applicable amount payable or Coupon value, local currency | N4+N..15 | AMOUNT |
| 3902 | Applicable amount payable or Coupon value, local currency | N4+N..15 | AMOUNT |
| 3903 | Applicable amount payable or Coupon value, local currency | N4+N..15 | AMOUNT |
| 3904 | Applicable amount payable or Coupon value, local currency | N4+N..15 | AMOUNT |
| 3905 | Applicable amount payable or Coupon value, local currency | N4+N..15 | AMOUNT |
| 3906 | Applicable amount payable or Coupon value, local currency | N4+N..15 | AMOUNT |
| 3907 | Applicable amount payable or Coupon value, local currency | N4+N..15 | AMOUNT |
| 3908 | Applicable amount payable or Coupon value, local currency | N4+N..15 | AMOUNT |

| 3909 | Applicable amount payable or Coupon value, local currency | N4+N..15 | AMOUNT |
|---|---|---|---|
| 3910 | Applicable amount payable with ISO currency code | N4+N3+N..15 | AMOUNT |
| 3911 | Applicable amount payable with ISO currency code | N4+N3+N..15 | AMOUNT |
| 3912 | Applicable amount payable with ISO currency code | N4+N3+N..15 | AMOUNT |
| 3913 | Applicable amount payable with ISO currency code | N4+N3+N..15 | AMOUNT |
| 3914 | Applicable amount payable with ISO currency code | N4+N3+N..15 | AMOUNT |
| 3915 | Applicable amount payable with ISO currency code | N4+N3+N..15 | AMOUNT |
| 3916 | Applicable amount payable with ISO currency code | N4+N3+N..15 | AMOUNT |
| 3917 | Applicable amount payable with ISO currency code | N4+N3+N..15 | AMOUNT |
| 3918 | Applicable amount payable with ISO currency code | N4+N3+N..15 | AMOUNT |
| 3919 | Applicable amount payable with ISO currency code | N4+N3+N..15 | AMOUNT |
| 3920 | Applicable amount payable, single monetary area (variable measure trade item) | N4+N..15 | PRICE |
| 3921 | Applicable amount payable, single monetary area (variable measure trade item) | N4+N..15 | PRICE |
| 3922 | Applicable amount payable, single monetary area (variable measure trade item) | N4+N..15 | PRICE |
| 3923 | Applicable amount payable, single monetary area (variable measure trade item) | N4+N..15 | PRICE |
| 3924 | Applicable amount payable, single monetary area (variable measure trade item) | N4+N..15 | PRICE |
| 3925 | Applicable amount payable, single monetary area (variable measure trade item) | N4+N..15 | PRICE |
| 3926 | Applicable amount payable, single monetary area (variable measure trade item) | N4+N..15 | PRICE |

| 3927 | Applicable amount payable, single monetary area (variable measure trade item) | N4+N..15 | PRICE |
|---|---|---|---|
| 3928 | Applicable amount payable, single monetary area (variable measure trade item) | N4+N..15 | PRICE |
| 3929 | Applicable amount payable, single monetary area (variable measure trade item) | N4+N..15 | PRICE |
| 3930 | Applicable amount payable with ISO currency code (variable measure trade item) | N4+N3+N..15 | PRICE |
| 3931 | Applicable amount payable with ISO currency code (variable measure trade item) | N4+N3+N..15 | PRICE |
| 3932 | Applicable amount payable with ISO currency code (variable measure trade item) | N4+N3+N..15 | PRICE |
| 3933 | Applicable amount payable with ISO currency code (variable measure trade item) | N4+N3+N..15 | PRICE |
| 3934 | Applicable amount payable with ISO currency code (variable measure trade item) | N4+N3+N..15 | PRICE |
| 3935 | Applicable amount payable with ISO currency code (variable measure trade item) | N4+N3+N..15 | PRICE |
| 3936 | Applicable amount payable with ISO currency code (variable measure trade item) | N4+N3+N..15 | PRICE |
| 3937 | Applicable amount payable with ISO currency code (variable measure trade item) | N4+N3+N..15 | PRICE |
| 3938 | Applicable amount payable with ISO currency code (variable measure trade item) | N4+N3+N..15 | PRICE |
| 3939 | Applicable amount payable with ISO currency code (variable measure trade item) | N4+N3+N..15 | PRICE |
| 3940 | Percentage discount of a coupon | N4+N4 | PRCNT OFF |
| 3941 | Percentage discount of a coupon | N4+N4 | PRCNT OFF |

| | | | |
|---|---|---|---|
| 3942 | Percentage discount of a coupon | N4+N4 | PRCNT OFF |
| 3943 | Percentage discount of a coupon | N4+N4 | PRCNT OFF |
| 400 | Customers purchase order number | N3+X..30 | ORDER NUMBER |
| 401 | Global Identification Number for Consignment (GINC) | N3+X..30 | GINC |
| 402 | Global Shipment Identification Number (GSIN) | N3+N17 | GSIN |
| 403 | Routing code | N3+X..30 | ROUTE |
| 410 | Ship to - Deliver to Global Location Number | N3+N13 | SHIP TO LOC |
| 411 | Bill to - Invoice to Global Location Number | N3+N13 | BILL TO |
| 412 | Purchased from Global Location Number | N3+N13 | PURCHASE FROM |
| 413 | Ship for - Deliver for - Forward to Global Location Number | N3+N13 | SHIP FOR LOC |
| 414 | Identification of a physical location - Global Location Number | N3+N13 | LOC No |
| 415 | Global Location Number of the invoicing party | N3+N13 | PAY TO |
| 416 | GLN of the production or service location | N3+N13 | PROD/SERV LOC |
| 417 | Party GLN | N3+N13 | PARTY |
| 420 | Ship to - Deliver to postal code within a single postal authority | N3+X..20 | SHIP TO POST |
| 421 | Ship to - Deliver to postal code with ISO country code | N3+N3+X..9 | SHIP TO POST |
| 422 | Country of origin of a trade item | N3+N3 | ORIGIN |
| 423 | Country of initial processing | N3+N3+N..12 | COUNTRY - INITIAL PROCESS. |
| 424 | Country of processing | N3+N3 | COUNTRY - PROCESS. |
| 425 | Country of disassembly | N3+N3+N..12 | COUNTRY - DISASSEMBLY |
| 426 | Country covering full process chain | N3+N3 | COUNTRY - FULL PROCESS |
| 427 | Country subdivision of origin | N3+X..3 | ORIGIN SUBDIVISION |

170

| 7001 | NATO Stock Number (NSN) | N4+N13 | NSN |
|------|-------------------------|--------|-----|
| 7002 | UN/ECE meat carcasses and cuts classification | N4+X..30 | MEAT CUT |
| 7003 | Expiration date and time | N4+N10 | EXPIRY TIME |
| 7004 | Active potency | N4+N..4 | ACTIVE POTENCY |
| 7005 | Catch area | N4+X..12 | CATCH AREA |
| 7006 | First freeze date | N4+N6 | FIRST FREEZE DATE |
| 7007 | Harvest date | N4+N6..12 | HARVEST DATE |
| 7008 | Species for fishery purposes | N4+X..3 | AQUATIC SPECIES |
| 7009 | Fishing gear type | N4+X..10 | FISHING GEAR TYPE |
| 7010 | Production method | N4+X..2 | PROD METHOD |
| 7020 | Refurbishment lot ID | N4+X..20 | REFURB LOT |
| 7021 | Functional status | N4+X..20 | FUNC STAT |
| 7022 | Revision status | N4+X..20 | REV STAT |
| 7023 | Global Individual Asset Identifier (GIAI) of an assembly | N4+X..30 | GIAI - ASSEMBLY |
| 7030 | Number of processor with ISO Country Code | N4+N3+X..27 | PROCESSOR # 0 |
| 7031 | Number of processor with ISO Country Code | N4+N3+X..27 | PROCESSOR # 1 |
| 7032 | Number of processor with ISO Country Code | N4+N3+X..27 | PROCESSOR # 2 |
| 7033 | Number of processor with ISO Country Code | N4+N3+X..27 | PROCESSOR # 3 |
| 7034 | Number of processor with ISO Country Code | N4+N3+X..27 | PROCESSOR # 4 |
| 7035 | Number of processor with ISO Country Code | N4+N3+X..27 | PROCESSOR # 5 |
| 7036 | Number of processor with ISO Country Code | N4+N3+X..27 | PROCESSOR # 6 |
| 7037 | Number of processor with ISO Country Code | N4+N3+X..27 | PROCESSOR # 7 |
| 7038 | Number of processor with ISO Country Code | N4+N3+X..27 | PROCESSOR # 8 |

| 7039 | Number of processor with ISO Country Code | N4+N3+X..27 | PROCESSOR # 9 |
|------|-------------------------------------------|-------------|---------------|
| 7040 | GS1 UIC with Extension 1 and Importer index | N4+N1+X3 | UIC+EXT |
| 710 | National Healthcare Reimbursement Number (NHRN) - Germany PZN | N3+X..20 | NHRN PZN |
| 711 | National Healthcare Reimbursement Number (NHRN) - France CIP | N3+X..20 | NHRN CIP |
| 712 | National Healthcare Reimbursement Number (NHRN) - Spain CN | N3+X..20 | NHRN CN |
| 713 | National Healthcare Reimbursement Number (NHRN) - Brasil DRN | N3+X..20 | NHRN DRN |
| 714 | National Healthcare Reimbursement Number (NHRN) - Portugal AIM | N3+X..20 | NHRN AIM |
| 7230 | Certification reference | N4+X2+X..28 | CERT #1 |
| 7231 | Certification reference | N4+X2+X..28 | CERT #2 |
| 7232 | Certification reference | N4+X2+X..28 | CERT #3 |
| 7233 | Certification reference | N4+X2+X..28 | CERT #4 |
| 7234 | Certification reference | N4+X2+X..28 | CERT #5 |
| 7235 | Certification reference | N4+X2+X..28 | CERT #6 |
| 7236 | Certification reference | N4+X2+X..28 | CERT #7 |
| 7237 | Certification reference | N4+X2+X..28 | CERT #8 |
| 7238 | Certification reference | N4+X2+X..28 | CERT #9 |
| 7239 | Certification reference | N4+X2+X..28 | CERT #10 |
| 7240 | Protocol ID | N4+X..20 | PROTOCOL |
| 8001 | Roll products (width, length, core diameter, direction, splices) | N4+N14 | DIMENSIONS |
| 8002 | Cellular mobile telephone identifier | N4+X..20 | CMT No |
| 8003 | Global Returnable Asset Identifier (GRAI) | N4+N14+X..16 | GRAI |

| 8004 | Global Individual Asset Identifier (GIAI) | N4+X..30 | GIAI |
|------|---|---|---|
| 8005 | Price per unit of measure | N4+N6 | PRICE PER UNIT |
| 8006 | Identification of an individual trade item piece | N4+N14+N2+N2 | ITIP |
| 8007 | International Bank Account Number (IBAN) | N4+X..34 | IBAN |
| 8008 | Date and time of production | N4+N8+N..4 | PROD TIME |
| 8009 | Optically Readable Sensor Indicator | N4+X..50 | OPTSEN |
| 8010 | Component/Part Identifier (CPID) | N4+Y..30 | CPID |
| 8011 | Component/Part Identifier serial number (CPID SERIAL) | N4+N..12 | CPID SERIAL |
| 8012 | Software version | N4+X..20 | VERSION |
| 8013 | Global Model Number (GMN) | N4+X..30 | GMN (for medical devices, the default, global data title is BUDI-DI) |
| 8017 | Global Service Relation Number to identify the relationship between an organisation offering services and the provider of services | N4+N18 | GSRN - PROVIDER |
| 8018 | Global Service Relation Number to identify the relationship between an organisation offering services and the recipient of services | N4+N18 | GSRN - RECIPIENT |
| 8019 | Service Relation Instance Number (SRIN) | N4+N..10 | SRIN |
| 8020 | Payment slip reference number | N4+X..25 | REF No |
| 8026 | Identification of pieces of a trade item (ITIP) contained in a logistic unit | N4+N14+N2+N2 | ITIP CONTENT |
| 8110 | Coupon code identification for use in North America | N4+X..70 | |
| 8111 | Loyalty points of a coupon | N4+N4 | POINTS |
| 8112 | Paperless coupon code identification for use in North | N4+X..70 | |

| | America | | |
|---|---|---|---|
| **8200** | Extended Packaging URL | N4+X..70 | PRODUCT URL |
| **90** | Information mutually agreed between trading partners | N2+X..30 | INTERNAL |
| **91-99** | Company internal information | N2+X..90 | INTERNAL |

## Works Cited

Boivin, Ryan. "Researcher Detects Ingredient Tampering." 29 09 2013. *The Star Phoenix, Saskatchewan.* newspaper article. 04 10 2013.

Canada, Government of. *CFIA guide to food safety.* 201. http://www.inspection.gc.ca/food/non-federally-registered/safe-food-production/guide/eng/1352824546303/1352824822033. 07 09 2013.

CFIA. "Recall Plans - Manufacturers' Guide." 12 08 2013. *Government of Canada, Canadian Food Inspection Agency.* document. 14 10 2013.

Government of Canada. *http://news.gc.ca/web/article-en.do?crtr.sj1D=&mthd=advSrch&crtr.mnthndVl=&nid=421539&crtr.dpt1D=&crtr.tp1D=&crtr.lc1D=&crtr.yrStrtVl=2008&crtr.kw=&crtr.dyStrtVl=26&crtr.aud1D=&crtr.mnthStrtVl=2&crtr.yrndVl=&crtr.dyndVl=.* 14 10 2008. web page. 01 10 2014.

Grocery Manufacturers Association, Covington & Burling LLP, Ernst and Young LLP. "Capturing Recall Costs, Measuring and Recovering the Losses." 2011. report.

GS1. *Web URI Standard.* 17 07 2019. https://www.gs1.org/docs/Digital-Link/GS1_Web_URI_Standard_i1_r_2018-07-17.pdf. 09 10 2019.

*GTIN Info.* n.d. http://www.gtin.info/. 08 09 2013.

Gupta, Manav. *IBM Blockchain for Dummies, IBM 2nd Limited Edition.* Hoboken, NJ, USA: John Wiley & Sons, Inc., 2018. ebook pdf.

IdentiGEN. "IdentiGEN launches DNA traceback program for Loblaw." may 2013. *www.identigen.com.* press release. 14 10 2013.

Institute of Food Technologists. *Global Food Traceability Centre.* n.d. article. 14 10 2013.

Low, Dr. *Professor* Judith Kirkness. 04 10 2013. phone interview.

Moroz, Bob. *President, RFID Canada* Judith Kirkness. 27 08 2019. email.

Nash, Kim. *Wall Street Journal.* 24 09 2018. https://blogs.wsj.com/cio/2018/09/24/walmart-requires-lettuce-spinach-suppliers-to-join-blockchain/#targetText=Walmart%20Inc.%2C%20in%20a%20letter,by%20Sept.%2030%2C%202019. 25 08 2019.

University of Guelph. *University of Guelph News*. 07 01 2019.
https://news.uoguelph.ca/2019/02/persistent-seafood-mislabeling-persistent-
throughout-canadas-supply-chain-u-of-g-study-reveals/. 25 08 2019.

University of Saskatchewan. *Putting a Trace on Food Fraud*. n.d. website article. 09 09
2013.

Made in the
USA
Lexington, KY